The Road To The Ultimate In Marriage

G. Michael Cocoris

© 2010, 2025 by G. Michael Cocoris

All rights reserved. This publication may not be reproduced (in whole or in part, edited, or revised) in any way, form, or means, including, but not limited to electronic, mechanical, photocopying, recording, or any kind of storage and retrieval system *for sale*, except for brief quotations in printed reviews, without the written permission of G. Michael Cocoris, 2016 Euclid #20, Santa Monica, CA 90405, michaelcocoris@gmail.com, or his appointed representatives. Permission is hereby granted, however, for the reproduction of the whole or parts of the whole without changing the content in any way for *free distribution*, provided all copies contain this copyright notice in its entirety. Permission is also granted to charge for the cost of copying.

Unless otherwise indicated, all Scripture quotations are taken from the New King James Version ®, Copyright © 1979, 1980, 1982 by Thomas Nelson, Inc. Used by permission. All rights reserved.

Exterior and interior design by John T. Cocoris

TABLE OF CONTENTS

Chapter 1
The Essence of Marriage   5

Chapter 2
The Ultimate In Marriage   21

Chapter 3
How To Love A Woman   33

Chapter 4
How To Please A Man   43

Chapter 5
How To Live With A Difficult Man   57

Chapter 6
How To Live With A Woman   73

Chapter 7
How To Prevent Juvenile Delinquency   85

Chapter 8
How To Rear A Juvenile Disciple   101

Table of Contents

Chapter 9
How To Head Off Unfaithfulness   111

Chapter 10
Family Finances   115

Chapter 11
How To Handle Marital Problems   137

Chapter 12
The Ultimate   149

Bibliography   151

About The Author   153

CHAPTER 1

THE ESSENCE OF MARRIAGE

Standing before a pastor, a man says, "I do." The woman he asked to stand beside him that day does the same. The pastor then pronounces them husband and wife.

Now, what actually happened? What is marriage? Is it legalized sex? Is it a socially accepted norm for bearing and rearing children? Can there be marriage without sex? Can there be a marriage without children? What is the essence of marriage?

I had been married for three years before I heard a definition of marriage. I was listening to a lecture on the home by Dr. Howard Hendricks when, for the first time, someone discussed the nature of marriage in any context. You can be married and not know what's happening to you and, more importantly, what is supposed to happen to you and your mate.

Granted, one can experience the essence of marriage and not be fully aware of what the essence of marriage is, but it is better to know about the substance of marriage for two basic reasons: First, if you have it, you need to know it so that you can maintain it. Second, if you don't have one, you need to know how to get one and enjoy it.

A psychiatrist once observed: "Inevitably, a large portion of my patients are people who have undergone the painful experience of divorce. As I listened to them day after day, year after year, explaining why their marriage failed, it gradually dawned on me that the vast portion of these unfortunate men and women have used divorce laws to amend a situation that had been confused from the beginning. They were victims of a failure to understand the real nature of marriage" (Michele Weiner-Davis, *Divorce-Busting*, 1992).

If failing to understand the fundamental nature of marriage can ultimately cause a divorce, it is imperative that married people know what the essence of marriage is. Henri de Toulouse-Lautrec, great as a painter but maladjusted to life, is reputed to have said out of the depths of his failure to find happiness, "Marriage is a dull meal with the dessert first." Is that what marriage is? What is the essence of marriage?

Marriage Is a Covenant

Genesis Marriage was first imagined, initiated, and instituted by God. He no sooner created man than He originated marriage. In the process of performing the first marriage, God described the essence of it. He said, "Therefore a man shall leave his father and mother and be joined to his wife and they shall become one flesh" (Gen. 2:24).

Some have erroneously concluded these words were spoken by Adam (Gen. 2:23), but the consensus of commentators is that this is an editorial comment by Moses. Other parenthetical observations by the author can be found in Genesis (Gen. 10:9; 26:33; 32:33). These were, of course, the words of God through Moses (Mt. 19:4-5).

God did not speak these words, nor were they recorded just for Adam and Eve. Adam and Eve did not have a father and mother! Instead, God is defining the nature of marriage as He designed it to be.

What, then, is God telling us about the essence of marriage? Plenty. This verse is pregnant with implications for marriage. For example, marriage is to be heterosexual, that is, between a man and a woman. Marriage is for Adam and Eve, not Adam and Steve. Marriage is to be monogamous. The text says his "wife," not his "wives." Jesus concluded that this statement implied marriage was to be permanent (Mt. 19:4-6). Later, in the Old Testament, polygamy and divorce were permitted in some cases, but neither was God's original ideal.

For our purposes, the question is: "What does this verse tell us about the *essence* of marriage?" For one thing, the statement describes an arrangement that could be called a social arrangement whereby a man and a woman agree to live together as husband and wife. It is social in that it involves more than the two individuals; it involves families, his family, and her family, and, no doubt, their friends and society. The two primary parties are agreeing to establish this arrangement. Our term for this is a legal contract. Marriage, then, among other things, is a legal contract.

Malachi This "legal contract" aspect of the essence of marriage is implied in Genesis 2:24. It is stated in Malachi. Malachi says that a man's wife was so "by covenant" (Mal. 2:14). The Hebrew word translated "covenant" means "pact, treaty, alliance." In other words, marriage is a legal relationship with legal responsibilities and ramifications.

What constitutes the legal aspects varies from society to society. In early Old Testament times, it involved an agreement between the groom's and bride's parents (Gen. 24). There was no wedding ceremony, so far as we know, but there was an agreement, a legally binding agreement. Later, in Hebrew culture, an elaborate ceremony was added. The ancient Romans and Greeks also had various types of ceremonies.

Throughout history, various rituals and ceremonies have been employed. Some would be strange to us. For example, there is an unusual marriage ritual among the Kwona of New Guinea. When a boy and a girl want to get married, the girl moves in with the boy's family but is not yet married. The purpose of this period is for the mother to decide how pleased she is with the girl and to see if she feels the son is pleased, also. The girl cooks her own meals while the boy's mother and sisters prepare food for the others in the household. When the mother feels that the time has come for the marriage, she tells the girl to prepare the young man's supper while he is away from the house. When he returns and unsuspectingly begins to eat his food, his mother announces that he is now married because he is eating the food his girl has prepared. Upon hearing this, the young man is supposed to rush outside, shouting how terrible the food tastes. This is the public declaration that he is now a married man! Once this public declaration is made, the couple begins living together as husband and wife.

For us today, the legal aspect of marriage consists of a license and a ceremony. The point is marriage is a legal contract. That's almost like saying the obvious, yet it must be said.

A woman whose divorce was about to become final asked Dear Abby if she should accept a ring from the next man she intended to marry before the divorce was finalized. Abby replied, "It is improper to become officially engaged until one is entirely free from prior legal commitments." Abby is right. Marriage is a legal commitment, a contract.

In an article entitled "For Better or Worst ... Mostly Worst: The State of Our Marital Unions," Chuck Colson writes, "Tina wants to get married, but her boyfriend Ted just wants to move in. Ted is an exceptionally honest young man, so here is what he says: 'Tina, I'm fond of you, and I want to live with you for the following reasons. First, it will make it easier for me to enjoy regular sex. Second, I want to protect my assets—assets I'd have to share with you if we got a divorce. Third, you already have kids, and I don't want to support them. Fourth, I'm waiting for my perfect soul mate to come along. Until I meet her, I'd like to live with you.'

"Sound convincing? Probably not. Tim's arguments are incredibly insulting. And yet, according to one study, these are exactly the reasons men want to live with women—reasons that not only insult women but make them big losers on the domestic front.

"At Rutgers University, researchers with the National Marriage Project published a report called 'Why Men Won't Commit: Exploring Young Men's Attitudes About Sex, Dating, and Marriage.' The study offers the top ten reasons men are reluctant to say, "I do." Among them: They can get all the sex they want without marriage. They want to enjoy their single life as long as possible. They want to avoid the financial pitfalls of divorce. And they're afraid marriage will demand too many changes and compromises. Apparently, their live-in girlfriends can get used to their bad habits or leave.

"Most galling of all is the admission by men that they don't want to marry their girlfriends because they're waiting for their "true love" to come along. *Then* they'll tie the knot, buy a home, and father kids. Meanwhile, their live-ins can pick up their socks and provide sex-on-demand.

"Grandma was right: Men won't buy the cow if they can get the milk free.

"Grandma was echoing the wisdom of the biblical writers. Read the Old Testament, and you'll get a picture of how carefully the ancient Israelites protected unmarried women: They knew how predatory, how utterly selfish men could be. Taking on the responsibilities of a wife and children involved hard work that would last a lifetime. And men were only motivated to shoulder those responsibilities because their culture demanded it.

"Modern women have far more freedom of movement than their sisters in the ancient world, but human nature is still fallen. This means that men are as predatory as ever—and women today are paying the price for it in a culture that doesn't demand marriage.

"I hope this report serves as a wake-up call to women who think men who want to cohabit have marriage on their minds. Most of them do not. Pastors ought to make this report the subject of a sermon. And if they know couples in their congregations are living together, they ought to encourage them to either marry—or separate.

"I hope you'll read the full Rutgers report. If enough women read it, maybe the day will come when men who invite women to live with them would get what they deserve: a slap in the face for that kind of insult" (Colson, "Breakpoint," 07/24/2002).

Marriage is Cohabitation

Marriage Marriage is more than a legal contract. It is the union of two people like no other union or relationship in life. Genesis 2:24 speaks of a man and his wife becoming "one flesh." Marriage, then, is not only a legal contract; it is cohabitation, sexual cohabitation. Whatever else "one flesh" may mean, it at least means the physical union (1 Cor. 6:16). At the end of a wedding ceremony, a pastor (or a Justice of the Peace) says, "I now pronounce you husband and wife." That pronouncement assumes that there will be a physical consummation.

Adultery This does not mean that sexual union and marriage are one and the same. Sexual relations do not constitute marriage, but marriage, by definition, involves sexual union. If that were not the case, adultery would no longer be adultery. It would be bigamy. To be precise, marriage consists of a contract and cohabitation.

Annulment Technically, there must be physical consummation before there can be a legal marriage. If there isn't consummation, there is no marriage. A license and a ceremony without consummation is not marriage. If there is no consummation, the law permits an annulment. It is not a divorce because the law recognizes there was no bona fide marriage.

I have known several people who have had an annulment. In one case, the couple lived in the same house for several months and the husband was found to be homosexual. The marriage was never consummated and thus was eventually annulled. In another case, a couple occupied the same house for several years, but she could not, or would not, participate in sex and the marriage was eventually legally annulled.

The Purpose of Sex This brings up the subject of the purpose of sex in marriage. What is the purpose of sex in marriage?

Roman Catholicism and even some Protestants have concluded that the purpose of sex in marriage is the propagation of the human race. While God has ordained that procreation be carried out in marriage (Gen. 1:28), and only in marriage, procreation is not the fundamental feature of marriage, nor is it the purpose of sex. Marriage is far more than mating, and sex is far more than a means to having children.

If the purpose of sex were procreation, then God would have had humans come into "heat," a mating season, like animals. The fact that humans have a constant sex drive argues that God intended sex in humans to be far more than mating.

The primary purpose of sex in marriage is mutual enjoyment. In a word, the purpose of sex is pleasure. Sarah, Abraham's wife, called sex "pleasure" (Gen. 18:12). The Hebrew word translated "pleasure" means "delight." The same root word is used to describe the joy of the Lord (Ps. 36:8).

Dr. Ed Wheat was a medical doctor who grew up in a liberal church. As an adult, he trusted Christ and devoured the Scriptures. A group of men conducting a marriage seminar asked him to speak on the subject of sex, which he did. Eventually, he became an authority on the medical and spiritual aspects of sexuality. He wrote a best-selling book on the subject and appropriately named it *Intended for Pleasure*. Sex is intended for pleasure.

In their book, *The Act of Marriage*, Tim and Beverly LaHaye say, "I have found many passages that touch on married lovemaking; some speak primarily about propagation, but many others prove that God intended the act of marriage for mutual pleasure. In fact, if the truth were known, it would probably have provided men and women with the greatest single source of married enjoyment since the days of Adam and Eve, just as God intended" (LaHaye, p. 14).

Marriage is Companionship

Genesis Marriage is more than a license for pleasure. Genesis 2:24 says a man is to leave his father and mother and cleave to his wife. The Hebrew word translated "cleave" means "to cling, keep close." It is used in the Old Testament of the bones cleaving to the skin (Job 19:20) and of the hand clinging to a sword (2 Sam. 23:10). Physical proximity is a prominent and perhaps even a predominant idea in the Word. Figuratively, it is used of loyalty, affection, and companionship. In this sense, clinging is not just physical.

For example, Moses writes that Shechem's soul "cleaved" to Dinah, the daughter of Jacob (Gen. 34:3, where "strongly attracted" is the same Hebrew word as "cleave" in Gen. 2:24). Indeed, the Old Testament exhorted the Israelites to cleave to the Lord (Deut. 10:20; 11:22; 13:4; 30:20; Jos. 22:5; 23:8; etc.).

The context of Genesis 2 indicates that God intended marriage to be companionship. God created Adam, observed him working in the garden, and commented, "It is not good for man to be alone" (Gen. 2:18). God then created Eve to be Adam's companion and helper.

Malachi Malachi confirms this conclusion. He says a wife is a "companion ... by covenant" (Mal. 2:14). The Hebrew word translated "companion" means "an associate, a partner." The essence of marriage is not just a contract or even cohabitation but a covenant of companionship.

What is companionship? Obviously, if there is to be companionship, there must be conversation. If there is to be companionship, there must be talk with the tongue or, in the case of deaf people, with hands, but there must be conversation.

The problem with many marriages is that there is no conversation at all. One illustration: Some couples have no conversation because they have a TV set. The wives in such marriages are sometimes called TV widows. One wife complained, "I can't get worried about whether there is life after death. I'd be satisfied if there was life after dinner." Today, it is the iphone, etc.

If you want to destroy a marriage, destroy the conversation. Silence will destroy a marriage because it strikes at the essence of it—companionship. Where there is silence, there is usually anger, hostility, or outright war!

Husbands, listen to your wives when they talk to you. Wives, when he asks, "What's wrong," don't say, "Oh, nothing."

Companionship is more than conversation; it is communication. While the problem with some marriages is that there is no conversation, the problem in others is that there is conversation but no communication. Talk is surface and superficial and anything but significant, or only one mate does all the talking, or both talk and neither listen. Like the lady who says to her husband, "I know you haven't been listening to me, for if you had, you'd have hit the ceiling by now!" Communication demands self-revelation. You must express how you think and feel. Communication demands listening. Your mate must understand your thoughts and feelings.

There are levels of communication. There is mouth to ear, as in, "Hi, how are you?" "I'm fine; how are you." There is mind to mind, as in "I have an idea I'd like to share with you," and the other person hears and understands. Then there is heart-to-heart, where one person shares his or her innermost feelings and the other understands the feelings and even feels with that person. The essence of communication at its deepest level is being able to share how you feel without your mate getting defensive.

Companionship is more than conversation and communication. In the finest sense of the term, it is comradeship. It consists of two people who share the same values and goals. They move together. They are, in the truest sense, partners. During World War II, a man joined the army to escape his nagging wife. When she continued to write him in the same contentious tone, he wrote back to her and said, "Honey, will you please quit writing to me? I want to enjoy this war in peace."

They had conversation and communication, but they had no camaraderie. Like the lady who told the marriage counselor, "Howard is an exceptional husband; he takes exception to my work, he takes exception to my friends, etc." Opposites attract, but opposites cannot hold a marriage together. You must develop common interests. That common interest may be your children, music, sports, a hobby, travel, etc. The ultimate is a common interest in and goal toward Jesus Christ (more about that later).

Husbands and wives need not approve of each other's traits or viewpoints but must agree on basic principles and goals. Failure to find common ground or to work out a satisfactory compromise places the marriage in jeopardy from the very outset. People divorce each other when they have "nothing in common."

Summary: The essence of marriage is that it is a covenant between a man and a woman to be each other's most intimate companion for life. Marriage is a union; it is the meeting of minds, hearts, and bodies, a blending of mutual respect, trust, and love. In short, it is legalized sex with friendship.

The Essence of Marriage

Are you married? The issue is not whether you have a license or do you have sex. The question is, do you have a marriage? Do you talk to each other? Are you communicating? Are you comrades? Are you friends? Do you have the real thing or a masquerade of marriage disguised as the authentic item?

Philip Dormer Stanhope, the Fourth Earl of Chesterfield (1694-1773), said, "Marriage is the cure of love, and friendship the cure of marriage."

In response to a woman in conflict with her husband, Ann Landers wrote: "The basis of a successful marriage is friendship. Too often, when a man and a woman marry, they are lovers—but not friends. Friendship means consideration for the other person's feelings, point of view, and integrity. It means trying to please, putting his wishes first. The woman who does this is going to find a more responsible, generous, easy-to-get-along-with guy. She will also find that he will insist on putting her wishes first. This is one piece of advice I can give with complete assurance that it works because it is born of personal experience."

Milo L. Arno once wrote, "What a pity! It was sure a beautiful friendship and meant so much to them both. Their personalities enriched each other, so they both blossomed into happy maturity and it was natural that they should want to enjoy each other for the rest of their lives. Marriage was God's plan, and their dreams had come true in it. It was a lot of fun planning their wedding, planning their new home, hunting for an apartment, and saying foolish things. They bought each other little surprise gifts and spoke with kind words, which meant so much. They were such good friends.

"Today, they have been married for a long time. It must be a long time from the way they act. They have not laughed together for a long time. They have not bought a little surprise gift or spoken an unusually tender, kind, or gracious word in a long time other than to say thanks or excuse me. They're good folks and they're getting along. They don't talk about divorce. They manage their business together, pay their bills, buy their household necessities, and are faithful at church. When she needs something, he tells her to go and buy it, and when he needs something, she does not fret when he buys it. They get along, but they have lost something. They are not the kind of friends they once were. Friendship should thrive in marriage. After the wedding, friendship can be enriched more than ever. Friendship can be planted in a wider field. There are more opportunities for togetherness, more chances for enjoyment, and more occasions when mutual helpfulness can enrich the friends who live together. There are more ridiculous things to laugh about, silly things to make fun of, and more occasions for having a good time. Friends who are married to each other can enjoy watching the moon rise and going for a walk while the stars come out. They can enjoy the thrill of each other's love and the excitement of love's richest intimacy. The gifts they gave each other can have a fuller, richer meaning, and the words spoken can be demonstrated and spoken from the heart. Many marriages would tingle with excitement and romance if the husband and the wife were the same kind of friends they were years ago. They would be careful to look their best for best for each other. They would go on dates. They would laugh at things that happened and could kiss each other at the door and still wouldn't have to interrupt the friendship's adventure by living in separate houses.

"Yes, a lot of fine friendships end in marriage. What a pity."

CHAPTER 2

THE ULTIMATE IN MARRIAGE

Owning a car is one thing; owning a Cadillac is another. Buying a boat is one thing; having your own luxury yacht is another. Being married is one thing; finding the ultimate in marriage is entirely different. What is the ultimate in marriage?

Some marriages could be called patriarchal because the husband/father is the ultimate authority. In such marriages, the husband is the ruler and the wife is often reduced to the status of a slave. All in the family are to bow to his whims and caprices.

Other marriages could be classified as matriarchal because the wife is the ultimate authority. Like the mother hen, the woman rules the roost and everyone, including the husband, is to fall in line and follow her. Your first reaction might be to think that the matriarchal type of marriage is practiced in primitive tribes in Africa, which is true, but it is also practiced in plenty of places in America. The father may appear king, but everyone knows the mother is the power behind the throne.

An old joke illustrates this well. A man was bragging to his buddies that he was the head of the house. "I make all the big decisions," he said. "My wife makes all the little decisions." "What decisions do you let her make?" someone asked. "Oh, she decides how the money should be spent, how to rear the children, and where to go on vacation." "Well," asked a friend, "what decisions are left for you?" "Oh," he said, "I decide big things like balancing the national budget and solving the tension in the Middle East."

Another possibility is anarchy. In this system, there is no ultimate authority. There are several forms of this concept. In some homes, no authority whatsoever is established. There are no rules. Everyone does that which is right in his own eyes. The result is anarchy. Another form is when the family decides that the authority should be changed. For example, in the book *The American Male,* Myron Brenton says, "True equality entails a shifting, fluid, dynamic kind of interaction in which leadership changes from one partner to another depending upon their specific interest in areas of competence and on specific contributions they are able to make in any given situation." He is saying is that there is no ultimate authority. These marriages never settle the basic question: who is in charge here?

Which of these concepts is the ultimate? What is the ideal in marriage? Who is the ultimate authority? The answer from God's point of view is found in Ephesians 5:22-29.

"Wives, submit to your own husbands as to the Lord. For the husband is the head of the wife as Christ also is head of the church and he is the Savior of the body. Therefore, just as the church is subject to Christ, so let the wives be to their own husbands in everything. Husbands, love your wives just as Christ also loved cleanse it with the washing of the water by the Word. That He might present it to Himself, a glorious church not having spot or wrinkle or any such thing but that it should be holy and without blemish. So husbands ought to love their own wives as their own bodies. He who loves his wife loves himself. For no one ever hated his own flesh but nourishes it and cherishes it just as the Lord does the church (Eph. 5:22-29).

Ephesians 5 is the most detailed discussion of marriage in the Bible. In it, God describes the ultimate, the ideal marriage. That is obvious from the illustration that is used in this passage. It is of Christ and the church. In his first epistle, Peter discusses marriage, but he deals with raw reality. He deals with the disobedient husband. His illustration is of a vessel, that is, a vase. Paul gives us the ideal and Peter discusses the raw reality. What does Paul say about the ideal, ultimate marriage?

Both are Converted through the Gospel

The fact that marriage is described in Ephesians Chapter 5 indicates that other material has been discussed before the passage on marriage. Thus, the passage on marriage in Ephesians 5 is based on the information in Ephesians chapters 1 through 4. It is a mistake, therefore, to plunge into Ephesians 5 without first going through Ephesians 1 through 4. One must go through the first four floors of a building to reach the fifth floor. What spiritual truths does Paul cover in Ephesians 1 through 4 that are assumed in Ephesians 5?

For one thing, Paul covers the subject of conversion. For example, in Ephesians 1:7, he says, "In Him, we have redemption through His blood, the forgiveness of sins, according to the riches of His grace." By the time Paul gets to Ephesians 5, he assumes both married partners are converted. Thus, the ideal marriage consists of two converted people.

Realize What must people do to be converted? First, they must realize they are sinners. The word sin means "to miss the mark." God has put a mark of righteousness, so to speak, on a spiritual wall. When measured by it, all humans miss that mark. God says, don't murder and don't hate. We've missed that mark. God says, don't commit adultery and don't lust. We've missed that mark. God says, don't steal and don't even covet. We've missed that mark. God says, don't lie and don't gossip. We've missed that one too. We've missed God's mark. In short, we are sinners.

Furthermore, we have become slaves of our sins. Jesus said, "Whoever commits sin is a slave of sin" (Jn. 8:34). We think, "I'll commit this sin this time and will choose whether I will ever do it again." Jesus taught that if you choose to commit it once, you become a slave to it and will commit it again. Habits are first cobwebs and then cables.

Recognize Second, people must recognize that Christ died for their sins. Ephesians 1:7 speaks of having redemption through the blood of Christ. The word redemption means "to buy back, to set free." Christ paid for our sins to set us free from our sins.

A. J. Gordon, a preacher of another generation, illustrated redemption by telling of a small boy selling birds on a street corner.

corner. He purchased one of the birds, took the cage around the corner, opened the door, and let the bird fly away. Gordon said he could almost hear the bird singing as he flew away, "redeemed, redeemed, redeemed." Just as A. J. Gordon bought and released the bird, Christ died to pay for our sins to release us from them.

Rely Third, to be converted, one must rely on Christ. Ephesians 2:8 says, "For by grace have you have been saved through faith and that not of yourselves. It is the gift of God." Faith is more than believing facts. It is relying on a person. When people realize they are sinners, recognize that Christ died for their sins and rose from the dead, and rely upon Christ to forgive them, they are said to be converted.

Thus, the ideal marriage of Ephesians 5 assumes the conversion of both the husband and the wife, as described in Ephesians 1 and 2. Have you ever been converted by relying on Jesus Christ to forgive your sin? If you have not or are unsure, you need to bow your head and tell God you want to trust Jesus Christ as your Savior.

Conversion can and should have a profound effect on marriage. For example, the gospel says, I am a sinner. I have a problem. For people to realize that and apply it to their marriage would have profound ramifications. When people have a marital problem, they usually think the problem is their marriage or their mate. They rarely say that they are the problem, but if they are Christians who have realized that they are sinners, they will begin by asking, "Am I the problem?"

Several small boys wishing to play a prank on an elderly man rubbed Limburger cheese on his upper lip while he was sleeping. When the man awoke, he took a whiff of the air and said, "The bedroom stinks." He arose, moved into the living room, sampled the air and concluded that it also stunk. He did the same in the kitchen. Then he went outside. Taking a deep breath, he exclaimed, "Oh no, the whole world stinks!" The problem was not the world, the kitchen, the living room, or his bedroom. The problem was under his nose. We tend to blame our problems on our mate or our marriage when what we should be saying is: "My problem is me."

Both are Committed to Spiritual Growth

The ultimate marriage of Ephesians 5 not only assumes that people have understood the concept of conversion in Ephesians 1 and 2 but also that they understand the concept of spiritual growth in Ephesians 4.

The Principle Paul says, "But you have not so learned Christ if, indeed, you have heard of Him and have been taught by Him as the truth is in Jesus. That you put off concerning your former conduct the old man which grows corrupt according to the deceitful lusts. And be renewed in the spirit of your mind. And that you put on the new man which was created according to God and righteousness and true holiness" (Eph. 4:20-24).

The basic mechanics of the Christian life in Ephesians 4 are summarized in the phrase "put off and put on." Believers are to put off the old man and put on the new man. The old man is everything a person was before conversion. In one sense, this old man was crucified with Christ the moment the person trusted Christ (Rom. 6:3-7). Speaking to the Colossians, Paul reminds them that they had put off the old man with his deeds (Col. 3:9). In another sense, this old life must still be put off (Col. 3:8). That's Paul's point in Ephesians 4:22.

No one does that all at once. If we could, we'd be perfect. Instead, this is the spiritual goal toward which we grow. So, let's call this being committed to spiritual growth (1 Pet. 2:1-3). Thus, spiritual growth includes putting off the old and putting on the new. These terms were used in taking off and putting on clothes. Imagine a man wearing a black coat. It is as if Paul is saying he should take off that black coat of sin and replace it with the white jacket of spirituality.

The Specifics Let's get specific. Paul says, "Let him who stole steal no longer but rather let him labor working with his hands what is good that he may have something to give him who has need" (Eph. 4:28). If a man becomes a Christian and stops stealing, would he be living the spiritual life? The answer is "No." According to this verse, he must *stop* stealing and *start* working so that he may give. Some get saved and stop stealing, which is good, but the process should not end at that point. Or, worse yet, they continue to steal but give some money away. Imagine a man in a black coat putting a white coat on over the black coat! Perhaps that explains why some are uncomfortable in their spiritual lives.

Let's apply this concept of spiritual growth to marriage. Paul says, "Let no corrupt communication proceed out of your mouth, but what is good for necessary edification that it may impart grace to the hearers" (Eph. 4:29). If partners were committed to spiritual growth, they would stop tearing each other down and they would start building each other up with their words. The grave of marriage is dug one dig at a time. Stop digging and start building. Don't tear down; build up. Stop complaining and start complimenting.

Both are Convinced of God's Government

The ultimate marriage described in Ephesians 5 assumes one other thing. It takes for granted that this is God's government for the home. These are neither Paul's ideas nor the church's nor mine. They are God's. In other words, the ideal Christian marriage assumes that both married partners are convinced of God's government in the home—God has the ultimate authority.

Not a Dictator Some feel that the husband is the dictator. They would argue that Ephesians 5 says that he is the head of the family and they interpret that to mean that he has all of the authority in the home. That is not Paul's concept of headship.

In 1 Timothy 3, Paul gives the requirements for an elder. In verse 4, he says the elder must rule his house well. The word translated "rule" means president. There is a difference between being a dictator and being a president. The difference is a constitution. The constitution in the home is the Word of God. The husband is not a dictator; he is a president who sees to it that the constitution, the Bible, is carried out. He is not to do his will;

he is to do God's will.

Not a Slave Likewise, some think that since the wife is to submit, she is an inferior slave. They feel God is saying she has no authority whatsoever. That simply is not true.

The Bible teaches the woman is to be the head of the house! Paul instructs younger widows to "manage the house" (1 Tim. 5:14). The Greek word translated "manage" is the one from which we get our word "despot." The wife is the despot over the house.

In other words, God is the head of Christ, Christ is the head of man, and man is the head of the woman (see 1 Cor. 11:3). More specifically, man is the head of the woman and the woman is the head of the house.

Shortly after I became a Christian, I heard Dr. Charles Woodbridge speak on the subject of marriage. At the time, I knew just enough to know that the Bible taught that the wife was to submit to the husband. When Dr. Woodbridge concluded his message, he said that his marriage was like a football team; his wife was the quarterback. I remember thinking that Dr. Woodbridge had departed from the biblical concept. Then he added, "And I am the coach." I was relieved that he returned to biblical orthodoxy but was surprised when he added, "And God is the owner and general manager of the team." Ah, that's the biblical picture.

Summary: The Ultimate In Marriage assumes that both married partners are converted through the gospel, are committed to spiritual growth, and are convinced of God's government in the home. In the ideal marriage, God is the ultimate authority in each heart and the home.

The ultimate is not a patriarchal marriage where the husband is the ultimate authority or a matriarchal marriage where the wife is the ultimate authority, nor is it anarchy where there is no authority. The ideal marriage is not a dictatorship, either of the husband or the wife; it is not a democracy, that is, the rule of the majority. The ultimate in marriage is a theocracy, the rule of God.

Oddly enough, the ultimate in marriage does not consist of two people; it includes three: a husband, a wife, and Jesus Christ. Furthermore, the man and the woman move more toward Jesus Christ than each other. It is then that they experience the ultimate. I once heard a professor illustrate this concept by putting two dots on the board about 18-24 inches apart. Each dot represented a person. He suggested that two individuals, especially in a marital relationship, try to move down that line to get as close as possible to each other, but they encounter a barrier. He then drew a third dot about 12 inches about the line and about in the center of it so that if the three dots were connected, they would have made a triangle. Then, he explained that the third dot represented Jesus Christ and suggested that the closer each individual got to Him on the triangle, the closer they got to each other.

The essence of marriage is companionship, but the ultimate in marriage is companionship in Christ. Without Christ, a couple can relate to each other mentally, emotionally, and physically, but in Christ, that same couple can share not only the mental, the emotional, and the physical but the spiritual as well. That is the ultimate.

The Ultimate In Marriage

Temple Gardner, as he was preparing for his marriage, wrote in his diary: "O God, that I may come near to her, draw me nearer to Thee than to her, make me know Thee more than her, that I may love her with the perfect love of a perfectly whole heart, cause me to love Thee more than her, and most of all that nothing may be between me and her be Thou between us every moment, that we may be constantly together, draw us into separate lonelinesses with Thyself and when we meet breast to breast, Oh God, let it be upon Thine own" (quoted by Haddon Robinson, November 1980).

CHAPTER 3

HOW TO LOVE A WOMAN

Husbands come in two extremes. On one end of the husband spectrum is "Bossy Bob." He is the dictator. Some dictator types feel that they rule by divine right. God, they would say, has put them in charge. Others would suggest that they rule by natural selection. Nature has given man the strength, size, intelligence, and initiative to be the ruler. So Bossy Bob runs the show, gives orders, and demands obedience.

At the other end of the husband spectrum is "Absentee Al." If Bossy Bob is the dictator, Absentee Al is the delinquent. He feels it is his wife and her house and children. In his view, he makes the money and she runs the house, so he buries himself in his business, goes off to play golf, and fishes with the fellows. That doesn't mean that he is absolutely absent. He does come around—when he needs something or wants something.

From a biblical point of view, a husband is not to be a dictator or a delinquent. What, then, is he to be? If he is to experience the essence of marriage, which is companionship, and the ultimate in marriage, which is companionship in Christ, what must he be like? God's instructions to husbands are given in Ephesians 5.

"Husbands, love your wives, just as Christ also loved the

church and gave Himself for it that He might sanctify and cleanse it with the washing of the water by the Word, that He might present it to Himself a glorious church, not having spot or wrinkle or any such thing, but that it should be holy and without blemish. So, husbands ought to love their own wives as their own bodies. He who loves his wife loves himself. For no one ever hated his own flesh, but nourishes and cherishes it just as the Lord does the church. But we are members of His body and of His flesh and of His bones. For this reason, a man should leave his father and mother and be joined to his wife, and the two shall become one flesh. This is a great mystery, but I speak concerning Christ and the church. Nevertheless, let each one of you in particular so love his wife as himself and let the wife see that she respects her husband" (Eph. 5:25-33).

According to the Scriptures, the husband is not to be a dictator or a delinquent but a devoted lover. A lover? What kind? Is he to be a Don Juan? No. What does God mean when He says that a husband is to love his wife? How does a man love a woman?

In this passage, Paul gives two illustrations of the kind of love God has in mind. A husband is to love his wife as Christ loved the church and as he loves his own body. From these two illustrations, three things are said about how a husband loves his wife. Here, Sir, are three ways to love your wife.

With a Sacrificial Love

Sacrificial Love Ephesians 5:25 says, "Husbands, love your wives."

The Greek word translated "love" means an act of the will whereby one does that which is best for the one loved. This verse also illustrates this love by pointing to how Christ loved the church. It says that Christ "gave Himself for it." In other words, this is a self-giving, sacrificial kind of love. It is not an emotional love, a sentimental love, or infatuation. It is an act of the will whereby one sacrifices himself for another.

Spiritual Needs Why did Christ love the church and give Himself for her? What was the purpose behind His sacrificial love? Paul says, "That He might sanctify and cleanse her with the washing of water by the word that He might present her to Himself a glorious church, not having spot or wrinkle or any such thing, but that she should be holy and without blemish" (Eph. 5:26-27).

These two verses contain three purpose clauses, each beginning with the word "that." The first one expresses the near purpose; the last two are the negative and positive aspects of the ultimate purpose. Consider Christ's three purposes for loving and dying for the church.

Christ died *so that* He might sanctify and cleanse the church. In the Greek text, "sanctify" is a verb and "cleanse" is a participle describing something that happened before the sanctifying. Christ died *so that* He might cleanse us from sin and set us apart to Himself.

The ultimate purpose of Christ's death is *that* He might present the church to Himself as a glorious bride. The church will be presented to Him at the Judgment Seat of Christ. He died that it might be a glorious, splendid, radiant bride. Her splendor is described as "not having spot or wrinkle or any such thing." There will be no defilement or disfigurement. There will be nothing to mar her beauty. The phrase "spot or wrinkle" is illustrated today in the washing and ironing of a gown. The bride will be bathed and her dress ironed to be presented in all her glory.

Put positively, Christ died *that* the church would be "holy and without blemish." Human brides prepare themselves for their husbands; Christ, the bridegroom, prepared His bride for Himself.

Thus, Christ loved the church and gave Himself for her to cleanse, to sanctify, and to present her to Himself. In other words, Christ sacrificed Himself to meet the spiritual needs of the church. He did not die to meet her physical need, that is, to supply a building for her to meet in, but He died for her spiritual need to supply her cleansing from sin and her separation to Himself.

Scripture The means that Christ uses to accomplish this end is "by the Word" (Eph. 5:26). There are a number of interpretative problems connected with the phrase "by the Word." To what is it connected? Is it connected to "sanctify," to "cleanse," or to the words "the washing of the water?" What does it mean? Is the word in this verse a reference to the Word of God, the gospel, or an oath at baptism? Is Paul saying that the purpose of Christ's death is to cleanse the church by hearing and heeding the gospel (1 Pet. 1:23, 25, where the term "word" is used in the gospel)? Or is he saying that the purpose of Christ's death was to sanctify the church through the Word of God (Jn. 17:17)?

Biblically, both are true. Christ cleanses through the Word, that is, the gospel, and He sanctifies through the Word, the Scriptures.

The question is, which truth is being taught in this passage? Some argue that the word order of the Greek text argues for the former, though the latter could be correct, and thus, this phrase is placed last for emphasis. Whichever interpretation of the verse is correct, this much is clear. The means Christ uses to meet the spiritual needs of the church is the Word of God. Christ gave Himself to meet the church's spiritual needs through the Word.

Keep in mind that all of this is an illustration of how a husband is to love his wife. A husband is to sacrifice himself to minister to his wife's spiritual needs through the Word of God. Practically, a husband must feed his wife spiritually from the Word, and he might have to sacrifice himself to do it.

Let's get specific. To do this, a husband must have time to *take in* the Word of God for himself. Most men are busy, incredibly busy. So, to accomplish this, he will have to sacrifice something. I know of one man who sacrificed some of his sleep time to spend time in the Word. He built a small room at the end of his garage, got up an hour earlier, and stole away to that quiet place where he could study the Scriptures.

For a man to minister to his wife's spiritual need, he must give out the Scriptures in manifesting the fruit of the Spirit and sharing the Word with his wife. Again, the problem is that many husbands are busy. So, he may have to give up something, sacrifice something, to spend more time with his wife. A man I know set aside Saturday mornings, that is, he made a date with his wife to take her to breakfast every Saturday. The children were old enough to take care of themselves when they awoke, and he had several hours alone with his wife every week.

The point is a husband needs to sacrifice himself to minister to the spiritual needs of his wife. He may have to sacrifice his time, his interests, or his desires to get into the Word and to give the Word to her.

When a husband does this, he establishes himself as his wife's head. Many pastors, counselors, and authors speaking and writing about marriage come to this passage and conclude that the husband is to be his wife's head, leader, and lover. Granted, this passage does teach that the husband is the head of his wife, but technically, God does not tell the husband that. He tells the wife that (Eph. 5:23)! All God says to the husband is that he is to love, but if he does what God tells him to do, he will establish himself as the leader. Any Christian wife would want to submit to that kind of spiritual leader. Who would not want to submit to a man who manifested the fruit of the Spirit as in love, joy, peace, longsuffering, kindness, goodness, faithfulness, gentleness, and self-control (Gal. 5:22-23)?

With a Sensible Love

Sensible Love The second illustration of how a man loves his wife is that he loves her as he loves his own body. Paul says, "So husbands ought to love their own wives as their own bodies; he who loves his wife loves himself. For no one ever hated his own flesh, but nourishes and cherishes it, just as the Lord *does* the church" (Eph. 5:28-29).

At first glance, it might appear that Paul is employing an

altogether different illustration. Actually, the two illustrations are connected. The word "so" or "thus" in verse 28 indicates that this illustration is connected to the preceding. The connection is that Christ loved the church, which is His body (Eph. 1:23; 5:23), so, in a like manner, a husband should love his wife because she is his body, or at least the two are one flesh (Eph. 5:31). Since a man's wife is like part of him, loving her is like loving himself.

In Ephesians 5:29-32, Paul seems to jump back and forth between the topics of husbands and wives and Christ and the church, but what he does is relatively simple. The unifying factor is the body. First, he applies the figure to husbands and wives (Eph. 5:29a), then he discusses that the church is Christ's body (Eph. 5:29b-32).

Paul draws two applications from the illustration of loving one's wife as one's body. He tells the man, in essence, that he is to nourish his wife as he nourishes his body, and he is to cherish his wife as he does his body.

The word "nurture" conveys the idea of feeding. Men love their bodies in that they feed their bodies. Some overdo it. I've seen men at potlucks pile food so high on their plates they needed sideboards to keep it from falling off. Most men, however, are sensible with their eating, at least they are supposed to be. They watch their diet and even exercise. This, then, could be called a sensible love.

Physical Needs The purpose of this love is to minister to the wife's physical needs. In practical terms, the husband is to feed his wife. Elsewhere, Paul teaches that if a man does not provide for his own, especially those of his own household, he has denied the faith and is worse than an unbeliever (1 Tim. 5:8). This also means clothing her and housing her. Every wife dreams of a bigger house, but she should at least recognize that her husband provides the house she has, and it is a symbol of love. A small house, which is a labor of love, is far better than a big house, which is the product of pride or a matter of materialism.

Wives should remember this truth. I've had wives tell me in counseling that they didn't believe their husbands loved them because they never *said* they loved them. While the husband should tell his wife he loves her, I have reminded these wives that one way a husband expresses his love is by working to provide for her. Of the three ways a husband is to love his wife, this is *one* wives should remember.

Husbands should forget this truth. That doesn't mean that they shouldn't do it. It means that after they do it, they should concentrate on other kinds of love. Some husbands tend to feel that they have loved their wives sufficiently since they fulfill this portion of love. That is not true. Of the three ways a husband is to love his wife, this is *only* one! So, Sir, do it and move on to the others.

With a Sensitive Love

Sensitive Love The second application of the body illustration is that a man is to love his wife the way he loves his body in that he cherishes his body. The Greek word "cherish" means "to heat, to warm." It is used in only one other passage in the New Testament. In 1 Thessalonians 2:7, it describes a mother's affection and concern for her child. This, then, is a sensitive love.

Did you ever see a man cherish his body? Did you ever see a man get sick? Many women claim that there is nothing sicker on the earth than a sick man. When a man gets sick, he is sensitive to the part of his body that hurts. He carefully and tenderly cares for himself or tries to get others to do it for him.

Emotional Needs The purpose of this kind of love is to minister to emotional needs. The word cherish highlights the emotional element, whereas the other words in this passage do not. To apply this kind of love practically, a husband must pay attention to his wife—daily. Many men work hard all day, come home, feed their faces, rest their bodies, watch TV, and ignore their wives. If you are sensitive, you will have to pay attention to your wife. When you come home, greet her with a smile, a warm hug, and whisper sweet nothings in her ear.

To do this properly, a husband needs to pay attention to his wife and notice details of her hair, dress, food, and house. You, Sir, need to notice those changes.

Whatever you do, use words. Donald Gray Barnhouse used to say, "Say it with flowers, say it with the dishrag, but whatever you do, say it with words." Tell her you love her when you get up in the morning, when you leave, when you come home, and when you go to bed. Use kind, warm, tender words to communicate your love to her.

Ladies, pardon the illustration, but men who live in a cold

climate will understand. Sir, in the winter, without warm attention, your car will grow cold and freeze. Is it possible that some men have cold wives who are frozen (frigid) for lack of warm attention? Why not use antifreeze and prevent all of that?

Summary: Husbands are to love their wives with a sacrificial, sensible, sensitive love. They are to minister to their wives' spiritual, physical, and emotional needs. If your house has no love, guess whose fault it is?

The problem is that wives are not perfect. After a man has been married for a few years, he finds her flaws, faults, and failures. The temptation is to focus on them. He begins to resent her. What he needs to do is love her despite her shortcomings. That's what Christ did for the church. He loved us despite our sins. A gospel song says, "He looked beyond my faults and saw my need." Likewise, the husband needs to look behind his wife's faults, see her needs and minister to them. Do you love your wife like that? I know you say you love your wife, but do you love her like that? Do you minister to her spiritual, physical, and emotional needs?

Howard Hendricks tells of a student who came to his office with a problem. The student said, "Prof.," as Hendricks is affectionately called, "I love my wife too much." The professor asked, "Is that right? Let me read you something." He read Ephesians 5, "Love your wife like Christ loved the church and you love your body." He asked the student, "Do you love your wife like that?" The embarrassed seminarian replied, "Well, not that much." "Then," said the professor, "You need to go home and do your homework."

CHAPTER 4

HOW TO PLEASE A MAN

The modern American woman is a rope in a tug-of-war. She is being pulled in different directions by various views of what a woman and a wife is to be.

For example, she is still being pulled in the direction of women's liberation. Several schools of thought exist within the women's lib movement. Some simply ask for equal employment and equal pay for equal work, which is long overdue. Others are demanding more—much more. They would say that just being a housewife is the lowest form of slavery, so hang the housework, cut the hair, burn the bra, and go by Ms. instead of Miss or Mrs. If you're married, keep your maiden name.

Or, she's being pulled in the direction of women's glamorization. This school of thought is not a movement but an ever-present pull. The message is to be glamorous. Start with a slim, trim figure. To get that, you need to exercise and drink diet soda. Then add the finest in fashion. Clothes, ladies, complement the charm. To top it off, style the hair: color it, curl it, comb it, clip it, or do anything to make it stylish. If you're wondering who's propagating this point of view, I suggest you watch television any night of the week, not the programs, but the commercials!

There are other pulls in other directions, such as the one that says a woman is to be all of the above. The question is, "What is a woman and a wife to be?" Is she to broaden her brain or beautify her body, or is the answer somewhere in between? What is the ideal wife like? How does a wife please her husband without being unhappy herself? God's answer is Ephesians 5:22-24. "Wives, submit to your own husbands as to the Lord. For the husband is head of the wife as also Christ is the head of the church and He is the savior of the body. Therefore, just as the church is subject to Christ, so let the wives be to their own husbands in everything."

Obviously, God is telling a wife to submit to her husband, a concept that has received a great deal of bad press. It is also a notion that has been misunderstood and misrepresented. What is the *biblical* idea of submission, and why does the wife have to do it and not the husband? Perhaps most importantly of all, how can the wife pull it off? A study of these verses in Ephesians 5 answers these questions.

The Wife is to Submit to Her Husband

What is involved in submission? I once took an informal, unscientific survey of Christian wives to determine their understanding of the biblical concept of submission. While traveling about the country, I quizzed Christian women who were Christian leaders, like pastors' wives, and women who were in the throes of divorce. Most said something like, "Submission means when you disagree, he wins." I responded, "Oh, I see. Before you can submit, you have to fight first." Most didn't think that was true, but they still didn't clearly understand the biblical concept of submission. How does a wife submit when there is no fight or even disagreement?

Respect In Ephesians 5:22-24, Paul speaks to women and, in verses 24-32, he addresses men. In Ephesians 5:33, he summarizes all that he has said. After reading what Paul has written, one would expect him to say that a wife is to submit to her husband and a husband is to love his wife, but that is not what he says. Instead, in verse 33, he says, "Nevertheless let each one of you in particular so love his own wife as himself and let the wife see that she respects her husband." Why did Paul say respect instead of submit? In his mind, respect is a synonym for submit, or at least respect is a part of submission.

Respect should not be a problem. A woman should marry a man she looks up to, one she admires. A husband should command, but not demand, his wife's respect. If he were the loving husband Paul described in Ephesians 5, a Christian wife would automatically respect him (and so would the children). When the husband/father acts respectably and the wife naturally respects him, the children grow up respecting authority.

Unfortunately, some men do not act respectably; consequently, their wives do not respect them. Peter deals with that raw reality in his first epistle, a passage which will be explained and expounded in the next chapter, but in marriages where the husband acts most of the time respectably, there will be those occasions when he does things the wife does not admire. How is she to respect him when he doesn't act very respectable? It may not sound romantic, but the answer is that she is to respect his position as a husband even if she doesn't respect his person at the moment.

Let me illustrate. When a man joins the armed forces, he is told he must salute officers. That does not mean he always agrees with them. In fact, he is told that he is saluting the position, not the person. The same is true for the president. If he were to come to town, the citizens might disagree with his policies, but they should extend respect to him due to his office. Likewise, a wife is to respect her husband, if not his person, at least his position.

Thus, at least part of what is involved in submission is respect. *The Amplified New Testament* puts it like this: "Let the wife see that she respects and reveres her husband, that she notices him, regards him, honors him, prefers him, venerates and esteems him and that she defers to him and praises him, and loves and admires him exceedingly."

A listener named Tammy told Dr. Laura Schlessinger, "My father's advice when I married was, 'You are marrying a man. Always treat him like one and he will always act like one.' Tammy says, 'I have noticed that in every area of our marriage, work, home, family, children, career, David excels when I treat him like a man. I mean by this that I do not demand he do things. I ask. I suggest options for his problems and then let him pick one. I never differ with him in front of the children. I do not deal with his family in an unpleasant situation—I let him deal with his family. I never do anything to embarrass him or make him feel less manly in front of his family, coworkers, children, neighbors, or friends. Let me tell you what this gets me. It gets me a man who is so comfortable with his masculinity that he can focus on being tender and loving and giving to me constantly because he is never concerned about protecting his ego or proving he is the 'man of the house' I do that for him" (Schlessinger, p. 163).

Schlessinger adds, "Showing respect for a husband in his own home not only sends him a message that he's loved and appreciated, but it also sets the game plan for the next generation's marriages. How much more important could it get?" (Schlessinger, p. 159).

Service There is more to submission than just respect. The word "submit" comprises two words: under and place. It means to place under. (Since that is the case, Dr. J. Vernon McGee advises single women to marry men they "look up to.") What is the point of placing oneself under another? Paul's illustration of a wife placing herself under her husband, that is, submitting to him, is of the church being placed under the Lord (Eph. 5:22). What does the church do under Christ? Among other things, she serves Him. Thus, submission is service. This should come as no surprise. God's original intent in creating Eve was that she should be a "helper" for Adam (Gen. 2:18).

A Godly wife has a servant's heart. This is not a put-down or a lowering of the wife to the status of a second-class citizen. Jesus Christ is our example. He said of himself, "The Son of Man did not come to be served but to serve" (Mk. 10:45).

I was once sitting in the living room of a close friend of mine when he called to his wife, "Honey, bring me," but before he could finish his sentence, she entered the room with what he was asking for in her hand. She anticipated his need. That's service. That's submission!

Some react to this concept. I've had wives say to me, "Do you mean I am to wait on him hand and foot? If he throws his pants on the floor, am I to go behind him and pick them up?" Once, in a small lady's Bible study, an older lady, upon hearing me teach this concept, exclaimed, "That's going too far. When my husband leaves his pants on the floor, I let them stay there. That will teach him to pick up his own pants."

Please do not misunderstand. I think a husband ought to be mature enough to pick up his pants but notice what that lady said, "I'll *teach* him." Instead of placing herself *under* her husband as a servant, she placed herself *over* him as a teacher.

Obedience There is more to submission than respect and service. The word translated "submit" not only means "to place oneself under," implying service but also obedience. To submit is to place oneself under the authority of another; in short, to obey.

Does that mean that a submissive wife is not entitled to her opinion? Does she have to be passive and silent? No! Submission is not silence, but it is obedience. A wife can speak: indeed, she ought to speak. When people submit to others, they place themselves under that other person. They put their talents, abilities, and insights at the disposal of others.

If your husband is doing something you think is not wise, tell him. However, once you have told him and the two of you have discussed it, there is a sense in which, according to the Scriptures, the ultimate decision rests with him and the Lord. So, if you disagree, say so that the two of you may discuss it, but what happens if you still disagree? There cannot be a majority vote. With two, that's impossible. Someone has to make the final decision. God says that someone is the husband.

That places a lot of responsibility on the husband. He is accountable to the Lord for his decisions and treatment of his wife!

Submission, then, includes respect, service, and obedience. Though this passage in Ephesians 5 was not written to tell a wife how to please her husband, if such instructions were followed, virtually all husbands would be pleased. (There are some men who, because of their problems, would not be pleased no matter what a wife did.) This chapter is entitled "How to Please a Man," not because that was Paul's intent but because that is the practical result of what happens when a person follows Paul's instructions.

Submit because it is the Divine Design

Divine Design Why does the wife have to submit to the husband and not the husband to the wife? The answer to that question is in Ephesians 5. In Ephesians 5:22, Paul instructs the wife to submit to her husband. Then, in verse 23, he says, "For the husband is the head of the wife, as also Christ is the Head of the church, and He is the Savior of the body." Notice verse 23 begins with the word "for," a Greek word that indicates that Paul is giving the reason in verse 23 for the command in verse 22. The wife submits to the husband because God has designated the husband as the head of the wife.

Marriage is a divine institution with a divine order. In the divine design, God has designated the husband as the head. Headship is leadership. Someone has to be responsible for seeing to it that the Will of God is carried out in the home. God says that someone is the husband.

Marriage is like a bicycle built for two. There are two seats, two sets of handlebars, and two sets of pedals, but only one can steer. The two riding the bike can talk about which way to go; if they want to maintain their balance and keep moving forward, they must cooperate. Nevertheless, only one can steer, the one on the front. In marriage, God says the husband is to sit up front; he is to steer.

This model for the husband-wife relationship often produces two great objections. Does not this pattern mean that the husband is superior? Secondly, does it not infer that the woman is inferior? The answer to both of these questions is "No."

Not Superiority Headship means leadership, but leadership does not indicate superiority. Part of our problem with the concept of headship is that modern Americans get their view of headship from the business world, where headship is dictatorship. The head of the corporation sits in the executive chair high above all those "under" him and gives orders. He is often a selfish, self-serving demagogue. The biblical concept of headship does not come from the business world but from the body. Christ is the Head of the church (Eph. 5:23) and the church is the body of Christ (Eph. 1:22-23).

What is the relationship of your head to your body? Well, for one thing, the head receives impulses from the body. For example, the foot may say to the head, "Hey, you need to know that I just landed on a tack. Move, the sooner, the better." The head responds and issues the order for the foot to move, even providing energy. A proper head provides sensitive, creative leadership. Notice verse 23 says, "Christ is the Head of the church and He is the Savior of the body." Likewise, the husband is the head and savior of the body who is "one flesh" with him (Eph. 5:28-31). He is to provide and protect, he is to bless and benefit, and she is to respond with submission and obedience.

Not Inferiority Does not this plan imply that a woman is inferior? She is to sit on the second seat of a bicycle built for two; she is the body, not the head. From a biblical point of view, headship does not indicate superiority. The body is not inferior to the head.

Consider the biblical illustration. Christ has a head. Paul said, "But I want you to know that the head of every man is Christ, the head of the woman is the man, and the Head of Christ is God" (1 Cor. 11:3). Notice that Christ has a head—God! Yet, the Bible specifically says that He is equal to God. Paul wrote, "Let this mind be in you, which was also in Christ Jesus, who being in the form of God did not consider it robbery to be equal with God" (Phil. 2:5, 6). It is possible to be a head and not be superior; it is possible to be under a head and not be inferior. Headship has nothing to do with being superior or inferior. It simply indicates that one takes the lead.

Suppose three people went into business together, each putting up $10,000.00 to buy a hamburger stand. All were equal partners. When the first customer arrived, all three approached the counter to wait for him. That wouldn't work. The three would have to get organized. One would become president, another cook, and the third would be the waiter. The president would take the leadership position. He would instruct the waiter to serve the customers and the cook to prepare the meals. In the board meeting, however, they would all be equal. They would be equal, yet they would have a head, a leader.

The reason that a wife is to submit to her husband is because it is the divine design. To accomplish anything, someone has to be the leader and someone has to follow. They may be equals, but one must lead and one must follow.

Service and submission would surely please any man, but it will certainly please God. A wife should submit to her husband, not just because it pleases him, but because it pleases the Lord.

Submit by God's Grace

The Problem Submission is tough. The sinful part of us, which, in the Bible, is called the flesh, resists and reacts to being told that we should submit to anyone, even someone we love. How is the wife to actually, practically submit to her husband? Paul concludes his words to wives and explains how to pull off what has been said: "Therefore, just as the church is subject to Christ, so let the wives be to their own husbands in everything" (Eph. 5:24).

Your first reaction to this verse might be that it doesn't help the situation. It only worsens it because Paul says that the wife must submit to the husband "in everything." Does that mean there are no exceptions? What if a husband, unlike Christ, asks his wife to do something immoral or illegal?

In this passage, Paul describes the ideal marriage as a loving, sensitive, responsible husband and a submissive, sensible, responsive wife. In that kind of relationship, submission to everything is not a problem. However, not all marriages are not ideal. In those cases, submission in everything can become a problem. Peter addresses the problem kind of relationship in 1 Peter 3:1-6 (see the next chapter).

The Solution Submission can become a problem, even in the best of marriages. How is the wife to submit? All believers face this problem, not just in marriage but in other relationships as well. The key to pulling it off is in the phrase "just as the church is subject to Christ" (Eph. 5:24).

How does any member of the body of Christ ever manage to submit to Him? The answer is only by God's grace. We are saved by grace (Eph. 2:8), we serve by grace (1 Pet. 4:10), and we suffer by grace (2 Cor. 12:7-9). Do we not also submit by grace?

All believers understand salvation by grace. The Greek word "grace" means favor. We were sinners in that we had broken God's law and pushed Him out of our lives. Yet, He did us a favor by giving us His Son to die in our place to pay for our sins. When we trusted Jesus Christ, we were forgiven and were given eternal life. In a similar fashion, believers are to live by grace by acknowledging that they have sinned and that they cannot save themselves from the current situation they are in. They acknowledge that they are self-willed and selfish and ask God to give them the willingness and the ability to be submissive. God responds, "My grace is sufficient."

A Seventeenth-Century pastor once said,

> Nature makes her a woman.
> Election makes her a wife.
> Only grace can make her subject.

Summary: A wife is to submit to her husband because it is God's design, and she is to do it by God's grace. Such a wife will surely please a husband, but, for sure, she will please God.

Shirley was married to a fellow who wanted to be a pastor. He attended seminary and then he and some others decided to start a church. Two of them went up in a small plane to survey an area, looking for land they might purchase. Unfortunately, the plane crashed and both men were killed. Shirley was now a widow with three small children.

She had known what it was to be a submissive wife and now she knew what it was to be separated permanently. She had known togetherness; now, she experienced loneliness. Deep in her heart, she wanted to be a wife, a submissive, godly wife.

In the providence of God, she was married a second time. Her second husband was a godly man engaged in full-time ministry. They both wanted to serve the Lord and do what the Scriptures told them.

After they had been married a short while, I had dinner with Shirley and her new husband. I asked Shirley to tell me what she had learned. Here was a woman who had been married in the will of God twice. She wholeheartedly wanted to be a wife and a mother. Now she had had that experience and I asked her what she had learned.

Her response surprised me. She said, "I've learned you can't do it without the Lord." Ladies, God will never arrange it so that you can do it without Him. If that's so, you will need Him to do what you need to and want to do.

CHAPTER 5

HOW TO LIVE WITH A DIFFICULT MAN

Over the years, on numerous occasions, I have had Christian wives talk to me about their non-Christian husbands. I have had them describe difficult, sometimes very difficult, situations. One wife has an unsaved husband committed to his business or consumed with his hobby. He is not interested in the Lord and even less in church. She wants to know how to win him to Christ. Another has an unsaved husband, who is not only not interested in spiritual things but worse. He doesn't like *her* going to church. Or, he wants her to go to parties and places like bars. It can get worse, much worse. Still another wife has a Christian husband who is not living for the Lord. He says he's saved, but he doesn't read the Bible, they do not pray together, and he doesn't regularly attend church. In extreme cases, he doesn't go at all.

The basic problem in all of these cases is the same. How does a Christian wife live with a man not living for the Lord? Peter answers that Christian in his first epistle. He speaks to wives about living with husbands who "do not obey the Word" (1 Pet. 3:1). Consequently, he is disobedient to the Lord and difficult to live with at home. What is the woman married to him to do? Peter tells her to do three things.

Be in Subjection

Peter says, "Wives, likewise, *be* submissive to your own husbands, that even if some do not obey the word, they, without a word, may be won by the conduct of their wives" (1 Pet. 3:1). The term "word" is a technical designation for the gospel. God has commanded all to believe in His Son so that they can be saved. To not believe in Christ is an act of disobedience (Jn. 3:36; Rom. 1:5). To disobey the Word means to reject the gospel.

Both Paul, who speaks of the ideal marriage, and Peter, who deals with the less-than-ideal, agree that a wife is to be submissive to her husband, but do they agree on what constitutes submission? The answer to that question is "Yes and no."

Respect Peter agrees with Paul that submission includes respect. He says, "When they observe your chaste conduct *accompanied* by fear" (1 Pet. 3:2). The Greek word translated "fear" in 1 Peter 3:2 is the same Greek word translated "respect" in Ephesians 5:32. It is no doubt, more difficult for the wife of a disobedient husband to respect him than it is for a wife of a devoted husband, but it is just as essential, and perhaps even more so, that she does it. If she maintains her respect for him, she is more likely to have an impact on him. The more she disrespects or despises him, the less influence she will have on him.

Dr. Laura Schlessinger opens her book, *The Proper Care and Feeding of Husbands*, with a quote from a letter from a husband, "I laughed when I heard the title of your new book. I thought, 'It won't happen. What woman would buy it? Who cares about us men? Men want a few things so badly that they would do anything for it. I think a good number of men want respect more than love. They like to feel they have some power: I nearly cry when you tell a woman caller to respect her husband. There is so much selfishness in the world—in marriages. Prosperity has allowed women to be so independent and thus so selfish. I always feel as though I come last—my feelings and needs come last."'

Signed, Edgar (Schlessinger, p. 1).

Service Peter agrees with Paul that submission includes service. Peter's illustration of a submissive wife is Sarah (1 Pet. 3:5-6). He tells wives that they are the daughters of Sarah if they "do good" (1 Pet. 3:6). The Greek word translated "do good" means to do well *for another's benefit.* If the wife of a disobedient husband sincerely serves him, she might win him spiritually. If she bosses him, she will lose him.

I know of a couple who had been married for seventeen years. He was a quiet, dedicated deacon, successful store owner, and henpecked husband. She was bossy, always telling him what to do because, as she said, "It's best for the family." One day, she told him he was getting up too late for breakfast. "Our daughter," she explained, "has to get up early to get to school, and I'm tired of fixing breakfast twice. So, why don't you get up and eat with us? Besides, it's best for the family. We can spend some time together at breakfast." Well, he got up, ate breakfast, and left. I mean, he left the house, left his wife, left his family, left his work, and never came back. The family broke up and the business went bankrupt. She bossed him and lost him. If she had served him, she might have won him. By the way, the last time I talked to her, she would have been delighted to fix breakfast twice daily if she could have just had her husband back.

Obedience Peter would agree with Paul that submission includes obedience. Remember, the word submission means "to obey," but Peter leaves no doubt that that's what he means by the word. He illustrates submission by pointing to Sarah, who was married to Abraham. He says, "Sarah obeyed Abraham, calling him Lord" (1 Pet. 3:6).

When married to a disobedient husband, the question quickly becomes, "Is there a limit to obedience?" Suppose the husband asks his wife to lie, for example, on their income tax return. Or, suppose he asks her to participate in wife-swapping. Is she to obey then?

Obedience to all God-ordained authority has a limit. Believers are to obey the government (Rom. 13:1-7), yet in the book of Acts, when the government told Peter not to preach or teach in the name of Jesus Christ, Peter replied, "Whether it is right in the sight of God to listen to you more than to God, you judge, but we cannot but speak the things which we have seen and heard" (Acts 4:19-20).

Does that limit apply to marriage? While this passage does not answer that question directly, one of Peter's statements seems to imply that there is a limit. He says that the wife is to conduct herself in such a way that her husband can observe her "chaste conduct" (1 Pet. 3:2). The Greek word translated "chaste" means "pure, free from defilement." One authority says it means more than just "cleanness." It suggests the notion of shrinking from contamination of a delicate sensibility to pollution of any kind. When a husband asks a wife to do something that is a clear-cut violation of the Word of God, she is not obligated to obey. However, she needs to make sure that it is a clear-cut violation of Scripture and not just something she doesn't want to do.

It is important—actually imperative—if a wife has to say "No" to her husband, she does so with the right attitude. Peter says the husband must observe her chaste conduct, "accompanied by fear" (1 Pet. 3:2). If a wife has to say "no," she must not do so with defiance but with a respectful attitude. She is to be righteous, not self-righteous.

A lady told a well-known preacher, "My husband wants me to go to bars with him. He does not get drunk; he just wants me to be with him, but I don't want to drink. What should I do?" He suggested that she go to the bar and drink a Coke. After all, Scripture does not say it is sinful to go into a bar. It does say it is sinful to get drunk so she could obey her husband without disobeying the Lord.

Silence Peter agrees with Paul that submission includes respect, service, and obedience; at the same time, Peter adds an element that Paul did not include. Peter says, "Likewise, you wives be submissive to your own husbands, that if any do not obey the Word, they *without a word* may be won by the conduct of their wives" (1 Pet. 3:1). For Peter, submission includes silence. In this context, he is talking about winning a disobedient husband, so the phrase "without a word" refers to being silent about spiritual things.

The phrase "do not obey the word" implies that the husband has heard the gospel, perhaps repeatedly, and has definitely and deliberately rejected it. Peter teaches the wife of an unsaved husband is to win him "without a word" (1 Pet. 3:1), which also seems to assume that he has heard the gospel and rejected it. The husband has heard the gospel either from his wife or someone else.

At any rate, Peter is addressing the wives of unbelieving husbands. If your husband has not heard the gospel, go home and tell him about the Lord, but if your husband has heard the gospel and has rejected it, there is another procedure to follow.

When a wife has a disobedient husband, usually, the first thing she tries to do is preach. She tells him he ought to get saved. If that doesn't work, she gets someone else to preach to him. She invites the pastor over or has a Bible study in their home. She leaves Christian literature around so he will see it. She turns on the radio to a Christian station or maybe goes so far as to put a gospel tract in his lunch.

That approach rarely works. Let me explain. Men are ninety-nine percent ego. A male has been defined as an ego wrapped in skin. Most men cannot stand for a woman to tell them what to do. So, wives, stop trying; just be silent.

Peter's point is that the conduct of their wives may win disobedient husbands. Wives, you will win your husband by your conduct, not by your conversation; by your life, not by your lip; by your walk, not by your talk. Ruth Graham said, "You make him happy; God will make him good."

A husband and some of his buddies frequently got together to drink and play cards. On one occasion, they were up most of the night when one said to the host, "Why don't we wake up your wife to fix us some breakfast?" The host said, "Are you kidding? She'd kill me." Another man in the group said, "My wife would do it and wouldn't mind." They, of course, thought he was joking, so he marched to the phone, called his wife in the middle of the night and said, "I'm bringing a number of men over for breakfast in a few minutes." Then, he invited the men to his home.

When the half-drunk men arrived, the wife was up and dressed, with her hair combed, and breakfast on the table for all the men. She waited on them as if their every whim were her command and said, "Sweetheart, I'm going back to bed. If you need anything else, just let me know and I'll be glad to get it for you." The men were shocked. When she left, they said to her husband, "How did you get her to do that?" And he replied, "Oh, she's a Christian. She does that all the time. She says she does it for the Lord." As a result of her conduct, one of the men in the group trusted Jesus Christ.

H. M. Stanley said of David Livingston, "If I had been with him any longer, I would have been compelled to be a Christian and he never spoke to me about it at all."

Some wives will object to such counsel. They will complain, "But my husband will not comply. He will only make life tougher for me." Granted, there may be suffering before success. In fact, Peter was aware of that. In this section of his epistle, he is talking about suffering. He tells the servants to "be submissive to your masters with all fear, not only to the good and gentle but also to the harsh. For this is commendable if, because of conscience toward God, one endures grief, suffering wrongfully. For what credit is it if, when you are beaten for your faults, you take it patiently? But when you do good and suffer, if you take it patiently, this is commendable before God. For to this you were called, because Christ also suffered for us, leaving us an example, that you should follow His steps" (1 Pet. 2:18-21),

Peter says that Christ suffered (1 Pet. 2:22-25), leaving us an example that as servants, we should follow in His steps (1 Pet. 2:18-21). Then he says, "Likewise you wives" (1 Pet. 3:1). In the context of 1 Pet. 3:1-6 Peter teaches that wives, like Christ and servants, may suffer if they submit. He also teaches that it's the way to win a wayward husband.

At the same time, as obedience in marriage has a limit, so there is also a limit to suffering. If a husband/father gets physically violent with his wife and/or children, the wife must take steps to protect herself and her children. This is a very serious situation. It is also criminal! After securing safety for yourself and your children, seek counsel from your pastor or a professional counselor.

Put on Godliness

After telling wives what to do, Peter advises them on what to wear. He says, "Do not let your beauty be the outward adorning of arranging the hair, of wearing of gold, or of putting on fine apparel, but let it be the hidden man of the heart with the incorruptible ornament of a gentle and quiet spirit which is very precious in the sight of God" (1 Pet. 3:3-4). In verse 3, he tells the Christian wife what not to wear and in verse 4, he tells her what to wear.

What Not to Wear First Peter 3:3 has been greatly misunderstood. Some have insisted that this verse means a woman should not fix her hair or wear jewelry. That is not what this verse means. Look at it carefully. It speaks about three things: hair, jewelry, and clothes. The word "fine" in the phrase "fine apparel" is in italics, indicating it is not in the Greek text. Peter speaks of arranging the hair, wearing gold, or putting on apparel. If he is forbidding the arranging of the hair or the wearing of jewelry, he is also forbidding the wearing of clothes. Verse 3 would be saying, "Live in a nudist colony."

In his day, many women overdid it. They were tempted to indulge in luxury and senseless extravagance. They thus called attention to themselves. They were attractive only in the sense that they attracted attention. Peter says don't do that. Don't concentrate on outward beauty.

What to Wear Peter's point is in verse 4. He says not to concentrate on outward beauty but to cultivate inner beauty. Outer beauty is a gift; inward beauty is cultivated. Outward beauty will not last; inner beauty will not be corrupted.

Peter says put on the incorruptible ornament of a gentle and quiet spirit. The Greek word translated "gentle" means "strength under control." It was used as a wild horse that had been tamed and was now under the control of a bit and bridle. The fashion that wins the top prize in the house of heaven is gentleness. The opinion that the Bible wants a woman to be is a spineless jellyfish is not true. The Bible desires women and wives to have strength and to have it under God's control.

In verse 1, Peter told wives not to say a word. That refers to spiritual things, meaning she was not to preach to her husband. Now, in verse 4, he tells her to have a quiet spirit, which refers to everything. She is to be silent about the Gospel and have an overall quiet spirit. In other words, the tenor of her life is that she is to have a quiet disposition. She should exhibit the tranquility that comes from trusting the Lord. Consequently, she will not be hostile, argumentative, aggressive, or domineering. She will not be bossy.

A man once called his wife Peg, although that was not her name. When asked why, he said, "Peg is short for Pegasus, who was an immortal horse and an immortal horse is an everlasting nag." A cab driver who worked in Atlantic City, New Jersey, where the Miss America Pageant was being held, was asked what he thought about all the beautiful women he had to haul in his cab. He replied, "There are a lot of good-looking ladies, but when they open their mouths, they spoil it all."

Precious in God's Sight At this point, I would expect Peter to say that if you have godly character, as in a gentle and quiet spirit, you will win your husband to Christ, but he doesn't. Instead, he says these qualities are "very precious in the sight of God" (1 Pet. 3:4). Peter says that the wife should not just look at her husband, but she should look beyond her husband to heaven. She should have a gentle and quiet spirit, not because her husband is watching but because God is watching. In God's sight, Such a wife is of great price.

The term "of great price" means very valuable, very costly, very precious. It was used of expensive clothes and ornaments. It is the same Greek word used in 1 Peter 1:7 of the blood of Christ. Think about that. God says that a woman who has a gentle and quiet spirit is of great price—she's expensive. For me to say that wouldn't mean much, but for God to say it means a great deal.

A pastor illustrated just how significant this statement is. He told me about going to Mexico City with a wealthy businessman. They went to an expensive restaurant for dinner. Tim looked at the menu and thought, "Wow, this is expensive." However, The wealthy man, not daunted by the prices, told Tim to order anything he wanted. They ordered an expensive steak. Then the waiter came with the dessert menu. Again, Tim thought to himself, "Wow, this is expensive." But a second time, his host said, "Order anything you like." When the check came, Tim's wealthy friend looked at it and said, "Wow, this was an expensive meal." Tim's comment was for him to say it was expensive was one thing, but for his friend, who had so much money, to say it was another. Well, it's not a poor person saying such qualities are of great price. It's God who owns everything!

Trust God

Holy Women After telling wives to be submissive and to have a gentle and quiet spirit, Peter gives an illustration. "For in this manner in former times, the holy women who trusted in God also adorned themselves being submissive to their own husbands as Sarah obeyed Abraham calling him lord, whose daughters you are if you do good and are not afraid with any terror" (1 Pet. 3:5-6). According to Peter, there is a long history and heritage of women adorning themselves with his recommended apparel.

Sarah He chooses one of the many pointing to Sarah, who was not only submissive to her husband, Abraham, but she obeyed him, even calling him Lord. That refers to Genesis 18:12, where Sarah heard that she was to have a baby and laughed, saying, "After I have grown old, shall I have pleasure, my lord being old also."

Someone will object, saying, "If I were married to Abraham, submission wouldn't be a problem. After all, he was the father of the faithful. He was a man of faith. He was godly. Submission to him would be easy."

Abraham may have been the father of the faithful, but he was a horror of a husband. It took him 175 years to grow up. Read Genesis and carefully consider what it was like to be Abraham's bride. On one occasion, he went to Egypt with his beautiful wife, Sarah. He was afraid they would kill him so they could have her, so he said, "Tell them you are my sister." That was partially true, for she was his half-sister. She obeyed.

Consequently, the king put her in his harem. That little trick by Old Abe almost got Sarah, his wife, into bed with the king. Had God not intervened, that would have happened. Nor is that an isolated incident. Genesis records that the same thing happened again. The women of the Old Testament, in general, and Sarah, in particular, are illustrations of women who were submissive to their husbands and who "trusted in God" (1 Pet. 3:5). The Greek text says they "hoped in God." The point is that these women looked to God, not to their husbands.

In a sense, this is the key. Wives, you must hope in God. Look to Him, trust Him. Faith is the key. Only as you trust God will you be able to be submissive to your husband. Only as you trust God will you be able to put on a gentle and quiet spirit. Only as you trust God will you be able to have an impact on your husband.

There are women's groups all over America: Daughters of the American Revolution, the League of Women Voters, etc. There are women's groups in the church: The Women's Missionary Circle, Women's Ministries, etc. The church needs to form a new women's group called the Daughters of Sarah, which consists of women who trust God to make them godly and submissive. Of all the women of history, who would you like to be? Helen of Troy? Cleopatra? Marilyn Monroe? Or Sarah? Sarah was the most beautiful of all. She was beautiful where it counts—in character. She trusted God and, therefore, she was godly and submissive.

Summary: The wife of an unbelieving husband is to be submissive and godly so that she might win him to Christ.

The vital element in this concept is faith. It will take faith in the Lord to live a godly life. It will take faith to be a submissive wife. It will take faith to win your husband to Jesus Christ. You need to believe the Lord, trust Him for a gentle and quiet spirit, a submissive spirit, and work in your husband's heart to bring him to the place of obedience to Jesus Christ.

In seminary, I was invited to conduct an evangelistic meeting in a church in Dallas, Texas. One night during the week, I spoke about the blind man Jesus healed. In that story, Jesus asked, "What do you want me to do for you?" At that point in the sermon, I said, "Think about that! The God of the universe asked this poor beggar what he wanted Him to do?" There was a lady there that night named Mrs. Capehart. She wanted more than anything to have her husband come to Christ. She had prayed for years that he might be saved, but that night, she decided she was going to trust God to save her husband. She even asked the Lord to save him on Sunday night.

Her twelve-year-old daughter trusted Christ during the week and was scheduled to be baptized on Sunday night. Mrs. Capehart knew her husband would come to see the baptism. As I walked into the church auditorium on Sunday evening, the pastor's wife stopped me and said, "Mrs. Capehart is here with her husband and she has brought clothes for him to be baptized." That night, I preached an evangelistic message and gave an invitation to come to the front to talk to us about trusting Jesus Christ. The first person down the aisle was Mr. Capehart. I had the joy of personally leading him to Christ, and after I did, I said, "Mr. Capehart, I did not know this until just a few moments before the service, but your wife has brought clothes for you to be baptized, and we have a baptismal service tonight. Would you like to be baptized?" He chuckled and said, "I might as well." When I returned to the church several years later, he was a deacon.

I am not recommending you pick a date and ask God to save your husband by that time. I am suggesting that if you are to be submissive, if you are to be godly, and if you are to touch your husband for Christ, you must walk by faith.

CHAPTER 6

HOW TO LIVE WITH A WOMAN

In school, we are taught that the universe operates on laws. These laws always work and they never change. For example, every action has an opposite and equal reaction. That's always true. So, we quickly learn that there are laws in science and rules in society. We also learn to cooperate with these laws and as we do, we discover that things function as we expect.

Then, we men get married and discover a whole new world—a woman's world. To a man, most women go through a period during which it is difficult to understand them. The period is between sixteen months and ninety-six years. Women do not operate according to laws. For example, right after you get married, you discover one day that your wife is crying. You think, "Oh, something is wrong." So you inquire, "Why are you crying?" And she replies, "Because I'm so happy!" To a man, that doesn't make sense. The "law" says you cry when you're sad, not, happy.

So the question is, how does a man live with a woman? How does a male live with a creature who is, in his estimation, unpredictable? God's answer to that question is in 1 Peter 3:7, which says, "Likewise, you husbands, dwell with them with understanding, giving honor to the wife as to the weaker vessel, and as being heirs together of the grace of life that your prayers be not hindered."

Actually, this verse is saying two things. A man is to dwell with his wife with understanding and, secondly, he is to honor her. Following those two injunctions are two phrases, both beginning with "as." In the Greek text, the first "as" phrase goes with "dwell with them with understanding," and the second "as" phrase goes with the command to give honor to the wife. Thus, Peter is saying that a man is to dwell with his wife according to knowledge as to the weaker vessel and he is to honor her as being heirs together of the grace of life. These two concepts form God's instructions for how a man lives with a woman who is his wife.

Know Her

Peter says, "Likewise, you husbands, dwell with them with understanding" (1 Pet. 3:7). A man is to dwell—that is, to live—with his wife with understanding. In short, he is to know her. There are a lot of jokes about men not being able to understand women. Many men do not understand women, yet God says a man should live with his wife according to knowledge.

Sir, you may not understand all women, but God says you are to know your wife. For starters, men and women are different physically, emotionally, and temperamentally.

Dr. Laura writes, "Men and women *are* different physically, psychologically, motivationally, and temperamentally. Anyone who has had exposure to babies and children can tell you that boys and girls respond differently to the world right from the start. Give both a doll and the girl will cuddle it, while the boy will more likely use it as a projectile or weapon. Give them two dolls and the girl will have the dolls talking to each other, while the boy will have them engage in combat.

"On my radio program, I have related an experience that vividly points out the subtleties of masculinity and femininity in parenting. I was at a swimming pool, watching a mom and dad play with their infant child. First, the mother, holding the baby against her chest, cooed to the baby and playfully swooped him up and down. After a while, she passed the baby to Dad, who immediately turned the baby's face outward and swooshed the baby forward and up into the air. My conclusion? Mom equals protection and nurturance. Dad equals autonomy and adventure. It is that perfect balance that helps produce a functional, secure human being" (Schlessinger, pp. 160-161).

There are several areas men should know about concerning their wives. Here are some suggestions. Others could be added to this list.

1. Gender. Though some would like to forget about it or deny it, the simple reality is that there is a fundamental difference between the sexes. For one thing, men are *basically* rational, and women are *basically* emotional. That does not mean, by any stretch of the imagination, that men are not emotional creatures and that women are not rational creatures. At the same time, men need to know and recognize there is an emotional side to a woman that they must understand if they are to dwell with her according to understanding. One ramification of this reality is that a woman needs emotional

assurance (so do men, but somehow it's different).

A man I know said that after he had been married about a month, his wife came to him and said, "Do you love me?" At the time, he didn't think anything about it and said, "Yes." A week later, she asked again, "Do you love me?" He thought it was strange, but he brushed his thoughts aside and said, "Yes, I love you." A week or so later, she came back again and asked, "Do you love me?" By now, He'd had enough. He sat her down and said, "Look, Lady, I love you and I'm going to prove it to you. First, I married you. Second, I'm still married to you. Third, I've not said a word about regretting marrying you. Fourth, I'm not planning on a divorce. Got it? I love you." It didn't work. Later, she still wanted to know if he loved her! In the years since, he learned she was not asking for information. She was asking for emotional reassurance. She wanted him to take her in his arms, hug her, and whisper sweet nothings in her ear.

Now, gentlemen, you need to know that about a woman. They are emotional creatures. They cry and when they do, you need to hug them.

2. Temperament. People are born with different temperaments. As everyone knows, there are extroverts and introverts in the world. The husband needs to understand his wife's temperament. If she is an extrovert, she will need and have a lot of friends. If she is an introvert, she will analyze everything. There are other possibilities. The point is a man needs to understand his wife's temperament.

3. Experiences. Beyond gender and temperament, all human beings have experiences that mold who they are. An early childhood

experience could make a person either like or dislike something. Husbands need to know what experiences have molded their wives. Did she have a loving father she respected or a father she didn't trust because he cheated on her mother?

4. Values. Much of who people are is rooted in their value system. Some women value wealth. Others value spiritual things more than material things.

Weaker Vessel Peter instructs husbands to dwell with their wives with understanding "as to the weaker vessel" (1 Pet. 3:7). What does Peter mean by weaker vessel? The word "vessel" means "utensil or instrument," like a household instrument. The Greek word was used of a vase. In Romans 9:23 and 24, this same Greek word is used of all human beings. Notice carefully, all humans are vessels.

The phrase in 1 Peter 3:7 is not just a vessel but a weaker vessel. Notice carefully that phrase implies that *all* humans are *weak* vessels. Men are weak vessels, and women are weak vessels. Peter is saying women are weaker than men. In his commentary on 2 Corinthians, Plummer says of this verse in 1 Peter, "Both husband and wife are articles of furniture in God's house and one of them is stronger than the other" (Plummer, p. 126).

That's a problem. How are women weaker than men? Certainly not spiritually or intellectually. You and I both know couples where the wife is as spiritual or intellectual as her husband, maybe even more so. Perhaps a case could be made for saying that women are weaker physically. There are differences in that aspect of the sexes. I think that the concept of a weaker vessel is simply saying that women are fragile. They are broken more easily. The truth is everyone has a breaking point. Husbands are to know where the breaking point is in their wives.

Let me illustrate. In your house, some vessels are containers. For example, in the kitchen, you have large, black metal pots that you could drop or even throw up against the wall and they would not be hurt. There are also vases, perhaps a valuable, hand-painted vase. It, too, is a vessel, but it is a vessel weaker than the pot. Men are to treat their wives like vases, not pots.

That means a man needs to know his wife and, specifically, he needs to know her breaking point. Do you know what hurts your wife? Do you know what breaks her heart?

I was speaking in a small, rural church in the Midwest. Since the church was small and could not pay the pastor a living wage, he had to take a part-time job to supplement his income. He drove a school bus twice every day, Monday through Friday. During the week I was there, he and I spent some time visiting, but he and I had to cut our activity short every afternoon so he could drive the bus. However, I noticed we actually got back twenty minutes earlier than we needed to so he could be on time. One day, I asked why he got back so early. He told me his wife was going through menopause and she worried about every little thing. If she thought he was going to be late for the bus route, she became very nervous and anxious, so he got back to the house before he needed to so she would not worry. That's dwelling with your wife according to knowledge.

Speaking of hurting your wife, it should go without saying that it is never acceptable for a husband to hit or otherwise physically injure his wife. It is extremely difficult, if not impossible, for virtually all wives to overcome being physically struck by their husbands. A woman who had seen the effects of spousal abuse in others told me, "A woman's emotional response to that treatment from her husband would resonate through her entire being and she would probably never forget it, even after he apologized and they patched things up (assuming that was the case).

Honor Her

Peter continues, "Giving honor to the wife as to the weaker vessel, and as being heirs together of the grace" (1 Pet. 3:7). Men are not only to live with their wives with understanding, they are to give them honor as being heirs together of the grace of life.

Heirs The phrase "grace of life" means God's gracious gift of eternal life. The Bible teaches that all humans, both men and women, are born spiritually dead, that is, separated from God. God's kind of eternal life was not in us when we were born. Jesus Christ, God's Son, came from heaven to die on the cross to pay for our sins so that we might be forgiven and be given eternal life. Because Jesus Christ paid for sin, God will give us the gift of eternal life (Rom. 6:23).

Now, Peter talks about the fact that a man and a wife are "heirs together of God's gracious gift of eternal life," which means that both men and women, husbands and wives, are saved exactly alike by trusting Jesus Christ. When they do, they are both recipients of the gift of eternal life (1 Pet. 1:3-4). Both, by Jesus Christ, have an inheritance in heaven.

Honor On one hand, Peter refers to the woman as the weaker vessel, so the husband is to live with her with understanding. On the other hand, she is an heir and, as an heir, the husband is to honor her. These two concepts balance each other. She may be weaker, but the husband will not use that knowledge to run over her but honor her. God says the wife is to be submissive to her husband, but He does not tell the husband to treat her like a subject. He is to treat her like an heir, giving her the honor due to royalty.

Your wife is royalty. She is a child of the King, not just any king, the King of Kings. He is not just the ruler over some small realm; He is the sovereign over all of the universe, and your wife, Sir, is His child.

The truth is that most husbands start out honoring their wives, but their honor grows less and less over the years. Someone has dramatized this degeneration in an article called "The Seven Stages of the Married Cold." It records a husband's reaction to his wife's cold during his first seven marriage years.

> First year: "Sugar dumplin', I'm worried about my baby girl. You've got a bad sniffle and there's no telling about these things with all of this strep going around. I'm putting you in the hospital this afternoon for a general checkup and a good rest. I know the food is lousy, but I'll bring your meals in. I've arranged it all with the floor supervisor."
>
> Second year: "Listen, darling, I don't like the sound of that cough and I've called Dr. Miller to rush over here. Now you go to bed like a good girl, please, just for me."

Third year: "Maybe you'd better lie down, honey, nothing like a little rest when you're feeling low. I'll bring you something to eat. Have we got any soup?"
Fourth year: "Look, dear, be sensible. After you feed the kids and get the dishes washed, you'd better hit the sack."
Fifth year: "Why don't you give yourself a couple of aspirins?"
Sixth year: "If you'd just gargle or something instead of sitting around barking like a seal."
Seventh year: "For Pete's sake, stop sneezing. What are you trying to do, give me pneumonia?"

Gentlemen, we are to honor our wives. Honoring your wife as an heir means considering her as a person, not just a possession. As a person, she has a mind. Honoring her includes honoring her ideas, opinions, and suggestions. Part of what I have done to honor my wife is to discuss things with her. I value and respect my wife's opinion. I appreciate her insights. I have taken counseling situations to her to get her evaluation. That's honoring her as a person with a mind.

Too many husbands dishonor their wives by doing things such as calling them stupid because they don't understand how a carburetor works.

When You Honor Your Wife, God Honors Your Prayers

At this point, I would expect Peter to say, "Do this, and you'll have a happy and harmonious marriage," but he doesn't. He gives the results all right, but it's surprising: "That your prayers may not be hindered" (1 Pet. 3:7). This is a surprise ending and a difficult phrase to interpret. It can mean one of several things.

Not Praying The phrase "that your prayers may not be hindered" could mean that you will not pray. That's true, isn't it? Did you ever get into a fight with your wife and try to pray? Not honoring your wife can stop you from even wanting to pray.

Not Praying Together It can also mean that you do not pray with your wife. That's true too, isn't it? Can you imagine at the end of a good fight saying to your wife, "Now let's pray" (maybe that's what we should do!).

Not Getting an Answer Finally, the phrase "that your prayers may not be hindered," can mean you will not get an answer. After all, the Bible does say, "If I regard iniquity in my heart, the Lord will not hear" (Ps. 66:18).

Which interpretation of this phrase is right? Perhaps all of them. Most would opt for the last one. Home life affects prayer life. A wrong relationship with your mate means you're in trouble with your Master. If you mistreat the King's daughter, you will not get what you ask from the King.

Perhaps, too, there is an implication from this statement that when a spiritual man is closest to his wife, he wants to pray.

Summary: A man is to live with his wife by knowing her, especially her breaking point, and he is to honor her because she is a child of God. If a man does not dwell with his wife according to knowledge and does not honor her, his prayers will be hindered. Failure in his relationship with his wife hinders his spiritual life.

This is practical advice, isn't it? Is it possible that Peter learned this in the crucible of experience? We know for certain that Peter was married (Lk. 4:38). One pastor concluded a sermon on this verse by suggesting that Peter learned the truths of this passage in his marriage. Perhaps Peter learned this truth one day when he came home from ministering in the public streets where he had been preaching all day and having a tough time because of the opposition. He was, no doubt, exhausted as he came into the house. Mrs. Peter was there working in the kitchen getting dinner ready. She, too, had had a frustrating day. Children can get on a mother's nerves. Not realizing that his wife had had a difficult time, Peter first went over to the stove, lifted the pot lid, and said, "What's for dinner?" He looked in and said, "Oh, no, fish again?"

Peter's wife, without a word, started sobbing, ran from the room to the bedroom, and slammed the door behind her. Peter probably thought, "What in the world did I say? I just asked what's for dinner. What's the matter with her anyway?" At the same time, he began to feel a bit remorseful.

So, Peter dutifully went to the bedroom door and knocked, but his wife from inside said, "Go away. I don't want to talk to you." Perhaps that shook him a bit and he took a walk. He knew just the person to talk to. As he began to pray, he sensed that something was not only wrong with his relationship with his wife, but something had interfered with his relationship with his Lord. He couldn't get through.

Then, the truth of this passage came crashing in on him. He realized he should have known how it would have affected his wife. He could have been more considerate when he came home. Finding a rose bush, he plucked one of its flowers and removed the thorns. Coming back into the house, he could still hear his wife sobbing in the bedroom. He opened the door and quietly moved to her side without saying a word. She was sitting in a chair, crying into her handkerchief. Without a word, he laid the rose in her lap. She looked up at him and, through the tears, smiled and said, "Oh, Pete, you shouldn't have," and he said, "I'm sorry, dear, I was thoughtless."

Then he said, "Let's pray together." This time, as he prayed, he felt that heaven's doors were flung open wide. Thus, Peter learned to instruct men to dwell with their wives according to knowledge and honor them, lest their home life interfere with their spiritual life.

CHAPTER 7

HOW TO PREVENT JUVENILE DELINQUENCY

When the two of you first discover there will be three of you, there is great joy and anticipation. When the little bundle arrives, there is excitement, but all the expectations and excitement fade away after a short time. The family settles down to the serious business of rearing the child.

Both parents know the child must be trained, and the training starts quickly. Mothers teach the child how to hold his or her own bottle. At about the same time, fathers teach their sons how to hold a football. So far, so good.

As the children get older, it becomes more complicated. It is more complicated for children because they have more things to learn. It is more confusing for the parents because they discover that they don't always agree on how the training is to be done. As a general rule, mothers complain fathers are too strict. "My husband is too tough on our son," complained one mother. As a general rule, fathers think that mothers aren't strict enough. Their opinion is that "If mothers controlled the children more, they would be better off."

On top of that, both parents worry about raising a child in our society. Some young people today even question whether or not they should have children because of the pressure of our culture. Children from the middle class and well-to-do families, as well as children from the inner city and ghetto, end up juvenile delinquents.

Many questions torment the minds of parents, especially those who are parents for the first time. Just exactly how does one go about rearing children? More specifically, how do parents today prevent juvenile delinquency? Since God is the ultimate authority of the home, let's ask Him.

He commands, "And you fathers, do not provoke your children to wrath but bring them up in the training and admonition of the Lord" (Eph. 6:4). Why does Paul address this injunction to fathers and not parents? Perhaps he has both fathers and mothers in mind. The word fathers can refer to parents (Heb. 11:23). Some have suggested that this verse gives the duty of parents, here represented by the father, but if Paul had meant parents, he would have said so. He used parents in verse 1! Therefore, when Paul addressed this verse to fathers, he meant fathers. Fathers are ultimately responsible for seeing to it that the instructions of this verse are carried out in the home. That does not mean that mothers should not follow this injunction. It means that the ultimate responsibility lies at the feet of the father.

This verse teaches parents how to "bring up" their children. In other words, how to rear them. Basically, it says three things.

Don't Provoke them to Anger

The text says, "Do not provoke your child to wrath." The Greek word translated "wrath" means "anger." Technically, there is a difference between wrath and anger in the Greek language of the New Testament. The Greek word for wrath means "hot anger" or an explosion of anger, while anger refers to a deep-seated feeling of resentment and hatred. The Greek word used in Ephesians 6:4 is anger, with a prefix added to indicate temporary anger. Thus, some have translated Ephesians 6:4, "Don't irritate."

How does a father or a mother provoke a child to anger? There are a variety of ways for a parent to irritate a child. Constant and unfair comparisons with another child or person will do it, but one of the major ways parents provoke their children to anger is in how they discipline them.

No Discipline No discipline will provoke a child to anger. Some parents do not discipline their children because they believe that discipline will hinder the development of the child's personality. Others don't care or are lazy. Children do not like that. They want rules.

In his book *Dare to Discipline,* James Dobson tells of an enthusiastic believer in progressive education who decided to remove a chain-link fence surrounding the nursery schoolyard. He thought the children would feel more freedom of movement without the visible barrier surrounding them. However, when the fence was removed, the boys and girls huddled near the center of the play yard. Not only did they not wander away, they also didn't even venture to the edge of the grounds. They wanted rules and discipline and when they didn't get them, they felt cheated and angry.

God goes so far as to say that where there is no discipline, there is no love. Proverbs 13:24 states, "He who spares his rod, hates his son, but he who loves him disciplines him properly."

I knew a university student who attempted to commit suicide. In counseling with her, I discovered that as a small girl growing up on a Minnesota farm, she felt that her mother didn't love her and she deeply resented it. In rebellion, she did things like pour a ten-pound bag of sugar on the floor or let her horse eat her mother's flowers. She told me she did things like that to see her mother react. She at least then knew her mother cared about something, but as far as she was concerned, there was no love from her mother to her and there was no discipline. Consequently, there was more anger, hatred, and ultimately a suicide attempt, which fortunately failed.

Too Much Discipline Too much discipline will also irritate a child. Some parents are convinced that their children need discipline, and they go at it with a vengeance. They over-discipline. They lay down too many rules and consequently, the children are disciplined too often. Parents must give their children rules and discipline them when broken. At the same time, parents also need to allow children the freedom to learn on their own.

In his book *Christian Living in the Home*, Jay Adams illustrates the distinction between what we must enforce as a rule and what children must be allowed to learn independently. He explains it this way. When a small child is old enough to discover a swing, it obviously fascinates him. He wants to learn to swing. It's everything to him. Mother wonders, "Is he old enough?" She knows he will get bumps and bruises at his age. There will be bloodshed, so she holds off as long as possible, but he begs.

Finally, the fateful day arrives. She puts him on the swing, tells him what to do, and what not to do. She helps him until he gets the hang of it, but she can't stay there all week. She has things to do, so she leaves. She grits her teeth and waits for the scream. When it comes, and it's bound to come, the child gets his lumps and learns from them.

On the other hand, the same child runs across the kitchen floor toward the gas range to grab that beautiful little flame. What does the mother do? Does she say, "Let him learn from his lumps?" Absolutely not. She quickly slaps his hand and says, "No!" For his sake, she keeps him from possibly serious danger. He might burn sensitive ligaments in his hand and disfigure himself for life.

The point is that parents must learn to distinguish between "swing" issues and "flame" issues. It is easy to do this when the children are small. It becomes more difficult later on. Parents need to discipline for their children's sake, but at the same time, they must not discipline them too much.

Some children suffer because they have never known restraint; others because it is all they have known.

Inconsistent Discipline There is another kind of discipline that provokes a child to anger: inconsistent discipline. Suppose a child is told, "If you do x, you will get punished." Sure enough, he does "x," but for one reason or another, he doesn't get punished. A few days later, he does "x" again. This time, the roof falls in, and he gets severely punished. If that is the order of the day, if there is no consistent discipline, it amounts to changing the rules day by day. The child never really knows where he stands. The child becomes confused when the rules are enforced only at the parent's whim. Such rules are the same as no rules.

When discipline keeps changing, the child is tempted to throw up his hands and say, "What is the use of trying?" Wouldn't you get exasperated with a baseball game if the rules changed daily? Imagine getting up to bat, swinging, missing twice, and being called out. And the next time, you discovered you had four strikes before you were out. The inconsistent application of baseball rules would provoke you with the game. Likewise, inconsistent application of the house rules will irritate a child.

Two other observations concerning provoking a child to anger need to be made. For one thing, Ephesians 6:4 says, don't provoke *your child* to anger. Some have said parents should never discipline their child in anger, meaning the parent should not be angry. Technically, the Bible never says that. Obviously, a parent should not always discipline a child in anger, but the Bible does not say that anger is a sin. Ephesians 4:26 says, "Be angry and do not sin." Furthermore, if a child did something that was a serious infraction of the rules and his parents got angry, it would be good for him to see the anger. He needs to know that some acts of disobedience are so serious it provokes his parents to anger. The test is whether it provokes *the child to anger*. If your anger provokes *him* to *fear*, fine. What the verse says is don't provoke him to *anger*.

The other observation is more of an implication than an observation. The admonition not to provoke a child to anger is obviously a negative command. Is it possible that behind that negative command is a positive concept? What is the opposite of provoking a child to anger? Is it not warmth and affection? Is there not a sense in which this verse teaches that the first rule of rearing a child is maintaining a good relationship with the child? If the child gets angry, the relationship is fractured, and the parent-child relationship will not function properly. On the positive side of this negative command is to ensure a good relationship between you and your child.

Train Your Child

Ephesians 6:4 says believers are to bring up their children in "the training and admonition of the Lord." The Greek word translated "training" means "instruction by correction" or "training by discipline." The Greek word rendered "admonition" means "to put in mind" or to "train by a word." The first of these words has to do with what parents do. The second has to do with what they say.

Rules Let's consider the first of these words, training, that is, instruction by correction. That concept implies there are rules. To properly train a child, there must be rules. Proverbs 1:8 says, "My son, hear the instruction of your father. Do not forsake the law of your mother." God has a law and so do mothers. The laws of God are moral issues. The laws of mothers usually have to do with manners, such as, "Don't jump on the sofa, don't run in the house, eat everything on your plate." Solomon's wisdom is that a child should learn to obey his mother's laws as well as God's.

The truth is we all have laws. The problem is that we keep retreating. Someone has described this in an article entitled "The Art of Strategic Retreat."

The parent begins by establishing a rule for neatness. The rule is that children are to put away their things. But then the parent retreat children must help their mother put away their things. When that rule fails, it becomes: When the mother has put away their things, they are not to complain that she has messed things up.

Or there is a rule about eating between meals. First, children are never to eat between meals. It then becomes: When you have a snack between meals, it must be only fruit or milk. Ultimately, it ends up: When they eat candy between meals, they must brush their teeth.

All parents start with a rule concerning bedtime. It usually begins with "8:00 sharp." Shortly after that, it becomes "not one minute past 8:30." Then it becomes "children who fall asleep while staying up late will not be carried to bed unless they wake up."

How about the rule for mealtime? At first, it is "children must clean their plates," then "no dessert for those who don't," and ultimately "absolutely no seconds."

Playing in the living room also demands a rule. The original reads, "Children must not play with glue or paint in the living room." That becomes "When playing with glue or paint in the living room, they must spread newspapers to catch spills," which evolves into "The children must say 'I'm sorry' when they don't spread a newspaper and spill glue or paint on the living room rug."

How about the rule for evening guests? The ideal is "Children must not get out of bed when guests arrive." The reality becomes, "Children may get up only to say hello." Perhaps closer to the truth is, "Children must say goodbye nicely when guests leave."

Then there's my favorite. The rule on watching TV. We start noble: "Children must not watch scary TV programs." That degenerates into "After watching scary TV programs, they may not sleep with parents." Ultimately, we say, "Children who must sleep with parents after a scary TV program may not bring the dog to bed with them."

Rod It should be apparent that all households need rules. Those rules should be few and fair. It should be equally apparent that there must be some form of discipline when those rules are broken. The concept of "training" a child in Ephesians 6:4, which means "instruction by correction or training by discipline," assumes there are rules and rules assume some form of discipline. Without discipline, rules will not work.

Proverbs 22:15 says, "Foolishness is bound up in the heart of the child, but the rod of correction will drive it far from him." Notice this verse says "foolishness," not "sin." The rod system of discipline should start early. James Dodson suggests at about eighteen months. If it is done correctly, it usually does not have to be done often.

If the rod is to be used effectively, as the Bible intended, it must be the first response, not the last resort. I once knew a pastor who had as well-mannered a group of children as I had ever seen. They were extremely well-behaved. The older ones were actively serving the Lord. After watching them for a while, I asked the pastor how he and his wife produced such well-behaved children. He told me, "You can train a child to obey you when you have given a command twice, or you can train him to obey you when you give him a command twice and raise your voice, or you can train him to obey when you have given him a command twice, raised your voice and threatened; or you can train him to obey you when you have said it once in a normal tone of voice."

Naturally, I was curious and wanted to know the difference between those things. He assured me that the difference was the point at which you apply the discipline. If the rod, or any form of discipline, is the first response and not the last resort, you will teach your child immediate obedience. If the rod is the last resort, you will train them to react rather than to obey. If it is applied as a last resort or is inconsistent, it will not be effective. Of course, the rod can be misused.

Admonish Your Child

Ephesians 6:4 not only talks about training a child by what is done but also about admonishing the child, which is training him by what is said. The Greek word rendered "admonish" means "to put in mind by words." Parents are to put in the minds of their children what is right and wrong. This kind of instruction includes several concepts.

Reproof For one thing, it involves reproof when that is required. In a sense, training and admonition go together. When you discipline by action, you should also discipline by word. Review the crime by asking such things as "What exactly did you do?" "Didn't I tell you not to do that?" "What do you think I should do?" and "Why is this wrong?" Before you put the paddle on the bottom, you should put the principle in the top.

Praise Training by word involves reproof when required and includes praise when you are pleased. Frankly, I think it is at this point that the battle is often won or lost. Many Christian parents only use correction in training their children. All some kids get from their parents is a spanking or a sermon. When the child goes to a public school, gets involved in sports, music, or academic studies, and does a good job, the teacher sincerely compliments him or her. When that happens, the child is drawn to that teacher. If the teacher happens to be against the Lord, the child will adopt the teacher's attitude towards spiritual things. The child may begin to drift in that direction simply because the teacher trained him or her with praise.

After a successful pastorate in a church for several years, a friend of mine was called to a larger church in a larger city. He and his family, including a teenage son, moved. After getting settled in their new home, the parents discovered that their teenage son was becoming very rebellious. He started failing in school and fighting church. The father, of course, became deeply concerned. He did everything he knew to do to correct the situation. Nothing worked. Finally, the father threw himself on the Lord. In his study, on his knees, he pleaded with the Lord for his son.

As he prayed, he wondered how God the Father handled His Son. Getting off his knees, he dug into the Scriptures and discovered the Father announced during Christ's earthly life, "This is My Beloved Son, in whom I am well-pleased." The pastor/father concluded that the statement involved at least affection and approval. "This is my Beloved Son," that's affection, "in whom I am well-pleased," that's approval.

He decided he would love his son no matter what and praise him whenever he possibly could. In a short time, his son was completely transformed. He started getting As and Bs in school. He lettered in football, track, and swimming. He even enjoyed going to church. I spoke in that pastor's church for a week and observed his son firsthand. It was when I asked the father how he produced such a disciplined son that he told me the story. There was no doubt in his mind that one of the major influences on his son's change from a discipline problem to a disciplined young man was how he had motivated his son and trained him with words.

Martin Luther advised, "Use the rod, but lay down an apple beside the rod."

Summary: Fathers are to rear their children by not provoking them to anger on the one hand and by training them with discipline and admonition on the other.

How To Prevent Juvenile Delinquency

The title of this chapter is "How to Prevent Juvenile Delinquency." How do we know that the concepts of Ephesians 6:4 will do that? From a biblical point of view, every child is a sinner. Left to himself, every child would become a juvenile delinquent. Love and discipline help prevent juvenile delinquency.

Some years ago, the Minnesota Crime Commission said, "Every baby starts life as a little savage. He is completely selfish and self-centered. He wants what he wants when he wants it: His bottle, his mother's attention, his playmate's toy, his uncle's watch. Deny him these things, and he seethes with rage and aggressiveness, which would be murderous if he were not so helpless. He is dirty. He has no morals, nor knowledge, no skills. This means that all children—not just certain children, all children—are born delinquent. Permitted to continue in the self-centered world of infancy, given free rein of his impulsive actions to satisfy his wants, every child would grow up a criminal, a killer, a rapist."

Dr. Gerald Davison, President of the New England Society for Adolescent Psychiatry and the Medical Director of a treatment center for violent youth in Portland Springs, Maine, says children become delinquent because they "miss out on nurturing love and affection ... youngsters need authority ... delinquent children are not helped by some idea of making up for lack of parental affection or by any system which reinforces beliefs that they are victims of society or of family wrongdoing."

Parents, you need to train your child. His future depends on it. You need to tell him what to do. His life depends on it. You need to teach him how to live. His happiness depends on it.

In 1944, a man in Hartford, Connecticut, took his children and several children from the neighborhood to the Ringling Brothers, Barnum, and Bailey Circus. They were gathered around him, enjoying the performance of the animals and clowns, when someone screamed, "Fire!" In an instant, a great part of the tent was ablaze. Women were screaming; children were crying. Men were shouting. Everyone was racing for the side of the tent. In that now-famous fire, 168 people died, and 500 were injured.

The man who had taken his children and his neighbors' children to the circus herded them to the edge of the tent and began pitching them out from under the tent as fast as he could. When he was sure he had them all outside, he collected them around him and raced from the burning tent. Gathering them together under a tree, he began to count heads. Suddenly, dismayed, he realized that his little curly-headed boy was missing. He was so sure he had all of them. Panic struck his heart and stomach. Leaving the children huddled and crying under the tree, he raced back to the flaming tent. By now, the whole circus tent was a mass of flames. The groans of the dying and the screams of others penetrated the air. It was an experience never to be forgotten. In agony, the man returned to the other children. Tears were streaming down his face. He gathered the children together and headed to the car.

Imagine how he felt. Put yourself in his place. Imagine walking up to the car. All the neighborhood children are clinging to your legs. As he did that, he discovered his little curly-headed boy sitting safely beside the car. Shocked, he said, "Son, what are you doing here? How did you get here?" Feeling he had done something wrong, the boy began to cry and explained, "Daddy, you always told me that if I ever got lost, I just had to go to the car. So I did."

Parents, tell your child what to do. His future depends on it.

CHAPTER 8

HOW TO REAR A JUVENILE DISCIPLE

The highest hope of Christian parents for their children is they will grow up to be God's children, not in the minimum sense of the word, that is, saved only, but in the maximum sense of the word, sold-out servants of Jesus Christ. The community is concerned about juvenile delinquents, but it is not enough for Christians to ask, "How can I prevent juvenile delinquency?" We must ask, "How can we produce juvenile disciples?"

If you are a Christian parent, I'm sure you've asked, "How can I, as a parent, rear a disciple?" Frankly, that's a big order. Children have minds of their own. Besides, in the final analysis, only the Holy Spirit can teach spiritual truths. Then, parents must pray. Nevertheless, parents play a part somewhere between the child's will and God's will. So, what is the parent's part in producing a juvenile disciple for Jesus Christ?

Perhaps we should begin by asking, "What is a disciple?" While many factors are involved in the answer, perhaps the simplest definition can be constructed from John 8:31. Jesus said, "If you abide in my Word, you are my disciple indeed." A disciple is a Christian who obeys God's Word. Thus, the question for parents desiring to rear a disciple is how to teach their child to obey the Word of God.

The answer is in Deuteronomy 6. "Hear, O Israel, the Lord our God, the Lord is one! You shall love the Lord your God with all your heart, with all your soul, and with all your might. And these words which I command you today shall be in your heart. You shall teach them diligently to your children and shall talk of them when you sit in your house, when you walk by the way, when you lie down, and when you rise up. You shall bind them as a sign on your hand and they shall be as frontlets between your eyes. You shall write them on the doorpost of your house and on your gates (Deut. 6:4-9).

This passage contains one of the Bible's most detailed descriptions of how parents are to rear their children. Furthermore, it teaches parents how to teach their children the Word of God. This passage contains three pertinent principles in producing a juvenile disciple.

Be an Example

The first principle that parents must master to produce a juvenile disciple is that they must be examples. Moses says, "These words which I command you today shall be in your heart" (Deut. 6:6). Then Moses adds, "You shall teach them diligently to your children" (Deut. 6:7). Before parents teach the Word of God to their children (verse 7), those same words must first be in their hearts (verse 6). In other words, they are to experience the truth of the Word before they teach it to their children. In doing that, they become an example.

What is involved in being an example? To what "words" do verse 6 refer? From the context, it is evident that several factors are involved.

Know the Lord For example, Deuteronomy 6:4 says, in essence, that one must know the Lord. The nations of Moses' day did not know the true and living God. They were polytheistic; they worshipped many gods. In their pagan darkness, God revealed Himself to Moses and this is what He said, "Hear, O Israel, the Lord our God, the Lord is One!" (Deut. 6:4). Deuteronomy 6:4 became the John 3:16 of the Old Testament. Even today, Orthodox Jewish radio broadcasts begin by quoting this verse in Hebrew. It is the Jewish revelation of the true God. Since God revealed Himself in Deuteronomy 6, the rest of the Old Testament has become complete. The New Testament has also been added. To know God today, one must trust His Son, who died for our sins and rose from the dead. When people trust Christ for the gift of eternal life, they know the Son and the Father.

Love the Lord There is more to being an example than just knowing the Lord. Verse 5 says, "You shall love the Lord your God with all your heart, with all your soul, and with all your might" (Deut. 6:5). If you love someone, you naturally want to spend time with that person. If that individual left town and wrote you a letter, you'd be eager to read the mail and even write back. That is our situation with the Lord. If you love Him, you'll want to spend time with Him, but obviously, He's not here. He has, however, written to us. The question is, "Do you read the mail?

Do you care enough to read what He has written?"

Obey the Lord There is another element in being an example: "These words which I command you today shall be in your heart" (Deut. 6:6). Obedience is the bottom line of discipleship. Love and obedience are related. In John 14:23, Jesus said, "If anyone loves me, he will keep My Word."

The point of all of this is that if you are to teach your child to be a disciple, you must be an example of a disciple. I once knew a Canadian girl who was the epitome of a gracious Christian. One day, I asked her how she became such a radiant Christian. She replied that it was her folks' example, especially her father. She said, "He really knew the Lord and loved Him. He was not very outgoing, but he was very consistent." Then she told me this story.

Her family once went from Canada to the United States—Detroit, to be exact—to do some shopping. While there, her father bought a small part for his automobile, which he could purchase for less in the United States. When the family arrived at the border to reenter Canada, the customs official asked if they had anything to declare. The father, of course, said yes. He was then informed that he would have to pay duty on that small part he had purchased for his car. The custom was so high he would have been better off if he had bought the item in Canada. So he asked if he could return the part. The customs official said yes, which is what he did. He then bought the part in Canada.

That experience made a profound impression on that girl. She told me that the part was so small he could have put it in his pocket and the customs official would never have known the difference.

Or he could have put it in the car, and they would have never discovered he had purchased it in the United States, but he didn't. His example helped produce a disciple in his daughter.

Some parents have saved money but, in the process, lost their kids. After I spoke on this subject, someone handed me the following article: "When Johnny was a little boy, he was riding with his father when a policeman stopped the car for speeding. The father tried an alibi or two and then tried a bribe. 'It's OK, son,' he told the boy, 'everybody does it.' When Johnny started school, his dad took him to football games, but he didn't buy the general admission ticket for him. 'He's not in school yet,' the father told the gateman. Dad took Johnny to a movie, too, but he paid for the child's ticket a couple of years too long. 'Everybody does it,' he assured the embarrassed youngster. Johnny listened with interest as the father whittled away at an income tax return, wondering why they claimed deductions they didn't have and reported donations they didn't make. 'You've got to do it to have anything left,' his dad told him, 'everybody does it.' On his way to school one day, Johnny got into a scuffle with the older boys and dropped and broke his glasses. 'It's all right,' his mother told him, 'We'll report them stolen and collect the insurance on them.' When he was sixteen, he got his first job in a food market. His assignment was to put the best apples, tomatoes, and potatoes on the top and the bruised ones on the bottom. 'Everyone does it,' his boss told him. Johnny barely got by in high school, but he was big and quick and made a pretty good guard on the football team. His best friend was little and slow, but he was a whiz at books and he helped Johnny pass. When the scholarships were passed out, colleges bid for Johnny but ignored his studious friend. 'All of them do it,' they told Johnny. When he was a freshman in college, he was approached by an upperclassman who offered to sell him the test answers. Johnny needed them badly. 'It's OK, kid,' the older boy said, 'everybody does it.' Johnny was caught using the illegal answers and sent home in disgrace. 'How could you do this to us?' demanded an indignant father and mother. 'If there is one thing the adult world can't stand, it's a kid who cheats.'"

Be sure your kids will check you out. They learn principles, but first and foremost, they imitate people. They close their ears to advice but open their eyes to an example. So don't expect your children to obey their earthly father if you, Sir, don't obey your Heavenly Father.

Be an Educator

Deuteronomy 6:7 says, "You shall teach them [the Word of God] diligently to your children." It then says, "And shall talk of them." These are two different activities: teaching and talking. Perhaps the teaching is a more formal kind of instruction, and the talking is a more informal kind. At any rate, to rear a disciple, parents must be examples and they must teach. In other words, they must be educators.

Characters Parents are to teach their children the Word of God. I only wish Moses had elaborated on just exactly how to do this. Unfortunately, he didn't. From my experience as a parent, let me suggest that you teach your children the Word of God commensurate with their age. For example, when children are small—that is, preschool ages 1-5—they love stories, so they teach children about the characters of the Bible.

Commands As your children get older, you need to teach them commandments. Between the ages of 6 and 12, children become command-conscious.

Concepts As the child gets older, the situation gets more interesting. What do you do when they become teenagers? It seems to me at that stage and age, you need to teach them concepts. Preschoolers are interested in who and older children want to know what, but teenagers insist on knowing why. So, characters or commands will no longer do. They want the concepts behind the commands. For example, during a trying time, they need to know that God allows trials to bring them to spiritual maturity.

Of course, all of this assumes the parents know the Word of God, even doctrine. If most fathers did not know more about their business than they did their Bibles, they would go bankrupt.

Be an Exposer

Deuteronomy 6:7 teaches that parents are not only to teach their children diligently, they are to talk. If to teach means that parents are to be educators, to talk means that they are to be exposers; that is, as parents move through the day, they are to expose their children to spiritual truth.

Sit Verse 7 instructs parents to talk about the Word of God as they sit in their house. When do you sit? Obviously, at mealtime. The mealtime should not be a church service. It should be a happy time with a great deal of laughing and hilarity, but mealtime is also a good time to informally and casually talk about the Word of God.

Walk Verse 7 also says that parents are to talk about the Word of God as they walk through the day. When this was written, parents were home more. They worked at home like farmers do today. There were no schools as we know them, so parents and children were thrown together more so then than now. Our problem is that we do not walk—that is, live—with our children.

You must find every excuse you can to spend time with your children. A father tells of making minor repairs around the house. He learned to wait until he could do it with his son. While working on some projects, there were plenty of opportunities to talk. If anything came up whereby he could teach his son some spiritual truth, he would do it.

For example, he tells of taking his son to a hardware store to buy what was needed for repairs. When he paid for what they needed, the clerk gave him too much change. The father said to her, "You did not give me the correct change." Thinking that he was accusing her of cheating me, she reacted. She was shocked when he pointed out that she had given him too much money. Once outside the store, the father told his son, "I could have kept it." Then he said, "I didn't because the Lord said you shouldn't." The father did not preach; he dropped it. The son *saw* the point.

Lie Down and Rise up Verse 7 also says parents should talk about the Word of God when they lie down and rise up. That's bedtime. You're to talk about the Word and to the Lord when you go to bed and get up. Children get used to this. It can become such an entrenched habit that there are times when they will not go to sleep unless their parent first prays with them.

Summary: To rear a juvenile disciple parents must be examples, educators, and exposers of the Word of God: when they sit, when they walk, when they lie down, when they rise up, that is, at mealtime, at bedtime, and anytime in every way.

Equally obvious is that this demands that you know God's Word and spend time with your family. If you go hunting *with* your son, you will not have to go hunting *for* your son. The ultimate question becomes one of priorities. Are your children high on your priority list?

A businessman was invited to speak for two hours for $400.00. He replied, "The price is right, the topic is right, but the day is wrong. I promised to take my two preschoolers to Disneyland that day and I can't break a promise." Most men would have accepted the invitation and postponed the trip to Disneyland. How high on your list of priorities are your children?

CHAPTER 9

HOW TO HEAD OFF UNFAITHFULNESS

The story is true. Only the names have been changed to protect the guilty. We'll call them Jack and Jill. They had been married for fourteen years and had five children. Jack owned his own business and was a respected citizen in the community. He even taught Sunday School. Jill was happy and content being a housewife and homemaker.

Then, suddenly, after fourteen years of marriage, Jack came home, packed his bags, said goodbye, and ran off with a girl much younger than himself.

How can such unfaithfulness be prevented? You may have never asked that question. You may even believe it could never happen to you, but I assure you it can happen to you, so you should be asking the question. Dr. Joyce Brothers reports that studies show that a man's mistress will frequently be very much like his wife. She also says that most people who have extramarital affairs don't initially meet their partners in a bar or a restaurant but at work. You see, it happens to people like you, so you need to ask, "How can I head off unfaithfulness?"

You may inject, "I'm a Christian; I love the Lord." I assure you unfaithfulness is no respecter of persons. It happens to simple saints and seasoned servants. It can happen to you, so you should be among those asking, "How can I head off unfaithfulness?"

There is a sense in which there is nothing you can do that will absolutely guarantee that your mate will never be unfaithful. After all, your partner has a sinful side, a subtle enemy called Satan, and lives in a sex-saturated society that offers many opportunities for sexual sins. Nevertheless, there are things a married person can do to help their mate overcome the temptations of the flesh, the world, and the devil. Granted, each individual is responsible for his behavior; nevertheless, the question is, what can the married partner do to help head off unfaithfulness?

The answer is in 1 Corinthians 7:1-7. "Now, concerning the things of which you wrote to me, it is good for a man not to touch a woman. Nevertheless, because of sexual immorality, let each man have his own wife and let each woman have her own husband. Let the husband render to his wife the affection due her and likewise also the wife to her husband. The wife does not have authority over her own body, but the husband does, and likewise, the husband does not have the authority over his own body, but the wife does. Do not deprive one another except with consent for a time that you may give yourselves to fasting and prayer and come together again so that Satan does not tempt you because of your lack of self-control. But I say this as a concession, not as a commandment, for I would wish that all men were even as myself. But each one has his own gift from God, one in this manner, and another in that."

To understand Paul's point, you need to understand the problem he is dealing with. Corinth was not exactly a paradise of purity. It was the sin city of the ancient world. Sexual looseness was not only permitted, it was promoted. The Temple of Aphrodite, the Goddess of Sex, stood on a hill high above the city. Since sex was part of the worship, the temple was served by a staff of temple prostitutes. Corinth was so sinful that its name became the word to describe sin in the extreme. A "Corinthian Feast" meant a despicable orgy. A "Corinthian drinker" meant an unrestrained alcoholic.

The situation in the city of Corinth affected the church at Corinth. Some of the saints were having problems with sexual looseness. Some of these were even visiting prostitutes. Paul deals with that in 1 Corinthians 5 and 6. Other believers, however, reacting to the moral looseness in Corinth, began ascetic practices, including celibacy. They decided that sex—all sex—inside and outside the marriage should be avoided. Therefore, marriage, they concluded, should be avoided and those married should abstain from sex.

The subject of 1 Corinthians 7 is marriage. Paul is answering the questions asked him by the congregation at Corinth. He answers the questions of whether or not it is okay for single people to get married and whether or not it is permissible for a believing Christian to stay married to an unbelieving mate. He also deals with the subject of sex within marriage and, in the process of doing so, tells us what we can do to help head off unfaithfulness.

Celibacy is Good

Paul begins, "Now concerning the things of which you wrote to me; it is good for a man not to touch a woman" (1 Cor. 7:1). The Greek word translated "touch" means "to cling to, to fasten to." This word does not refer to shaking hands, hugging, or dancing. It is a euphemism for sexual intercourse; it appears in classical Greek and the Septuagint as a figurative expression for sexual intercourse itself. Perhaps this statement, "It is good for a man not to touch a woman," was a slogan of the ascetics at Corinth. Their view was that it was good for a man to abstain from sexual relations with a woman, and. therefore, they taught, "Don't get married and if you get married, abstain from sex." According to them, celibacy was preferable and, perhaps, even compulsory.

While the primary reference to the word "touch" is to sex itself, in this context, there is no doubt that Paul is saying more than it is good for a man to abstain from sexual intercourse with a woman. He is saying it is good for a man not to get married. In other words, celibacy is good. It is evident that is his meaning here because, in the next verse, he says, "Nevertheless, because of sexual immorality, let each man have his own wife, and let each woman have her own husband" (1 Cor. 7:2). The New International Version (a paraphrase) translates this verse: "It is good for a man not to marry."

Why does Paul say that celibacy is good? Candidly, he does not answer that question, at least in this verse, but later in this chapter, he gives several reasons why a person should stay single.

For example, he says, "Now concerning virgins, I have no commandment from the Lord. Yet, I give judgment as one whom the Lord. in His mercy. has made trustworthy. I suppose, therefore, that this is good because of the present distress—that it is good for a man to remain as he is" (1 Cor. 7:25-26). Paul is saying that because of the "present distress," it might be best to stay single. No one knows the meaning of "present distress." Maybe it was the persecution of Christians. Whatever it was, his teaching could include that a crisis in the world is a reason for staying single.

That is true today. Crises periodically appear, which could be a reason for now getting married. War might be an example. Suppose a young man had been drafted, finished boot camp, and was about to be shipped to the front lines. In that situation, waiting until he returns to get married might be best.

Or take a money crisis. When speaking at a Bible college, a student came to me for counsel. He said he and his girl wanted to get married very severely, and he also wanted to go to seminary, but they had a problem. He owed thousands of dollars on school bills. He wanted to know if he should 1) pay off the bills first and then get married or 2) get married and then pay off the bills.

I told him that money problems were one of the chief causes of marital difficulties and divorce in the United States. Financial failure can spell marriage failure. So, I asked him what he could do to earn money. He replied that his father was working on the Alaska Pipeline, which was being constructed. He informed me that he could get a job earning $10,000 in six months (a lot of money then). I advised him, by all means, to do just that. I can imagine him being on the pipeline talking about his girlfriend and someone asking him, "If you're that much in love, why don't you get married?" And he would answer, "Because of the present distress."

There is another reason for not getting married. Paul says, "But I want you to be without care. He who is unmarried cares for the things that belong to the Lord, and how he may please the Lord, but he who is married cares about the things of the world, and how he may please his wife" (1 Cor. 7:32-33), Here, Paul is saying that if you're married you'll have the cares of marriage to occupy your time, but if you're single, you'll be free to spend more time serving the Lord.

If you have a deep desire to serve the Lord, this could greatly appeal to you, but before jumping into the waters of celibacy, you need to know how to swim—alone. Frankly, not everyone can do that. Even the Apostle Paul warns, "I wish that all men were even as myself, but each one has his own gift from God, one in this manner and another in that" (1 Cor. 7:7).

The point is marriage is the norm and celibacy is the exception. Not being the norm, celibacy requires a special gift from God. Nevertheless, celibacy, if you have the gift, is good.

Marriage Prevents Fornication

After establishing that celibacy is permissible, Paul adds, "Nevertheless, because of sexual immorality, let each man have his own wife, and let each woman have her own husband" (1 Cor.

7:2). The point is straightforward. To avoid sexual immorality, get married. Marriage prevents sexual sins.

Some have criticized Paul for saying this. They say his view of marriage is low if the only reason to get married is to prevent sexual immorality. Paul did not have a low view of marriage; he had a realistic view of people. He would say there is more involved. There are more reasons for marriage, but this is part of the picture. In 1 Corinthians 7:9, he says, "If they cannot exercise self-control, let them marry. It is better to marry than to burn with passion."

While speaking at a Bible conference, a young man who had been married for only a few months came to talk to me. He told me he was in a Christian college preparing for the ministry when he fell in love. He and his girl loved each other very much and planned to marry. In the meantime, they were getting more and more involved physically, so before they got into fornication, they decided to push up the wedding date and get married, which they did. Now, after being married, he felt guilty because the reason he got married when he did was to prevent sexual immorality. I shared with him that Paul said it was a good idea and not to feel guilty. He was greatly relieved.

I also recall a girl saying to me once, "I have been asked to be a bridesmaid in my girlfriend's wedding, but she and her fiancée are getting married a year earlier than they planned just because of sex. I disapprove of that. Should I be in the wedding? If I am, am I showing my approval?" I informed her that Paul would have supported them getting married early. As a result of our conversation, she participated in the wedding.

Someone will object: "Wait a minute. Marriage doesn't always prevent sexual immorality. How can Paul say marriage prevents sexual sins? There must be more."

Marriage Prevents Immorality if You Pay Your Marital Debt

There is more. Paul says, "Let the husband render to his wife the affection due her and likewise also the wife to her husband" (1 Cor. 7:3). The Greek word translated "due" means just that: "to owe." The same word is used in Matthew 18:28 for owing money. Affection, of course, in this context, is more than hugging and kissing. It includes sexual intercourse. Paul is saying that sex in marriage is an obligation and a responsibility. It's like owing money. It is a debt to be paid.

Some look at sex in marriage as a favor. The Bible teaches that it is not a favor but an obligation. Worse yet, some view sex in marriage as a reward. I've had men tell me things like, "My wife's attitude toward sex is that if you mow the lawn or fix the faucet, I'll reward you tonight." Sex is not a reward. In marriage, it is an obligation. Perhaps worst of all, some think of it as a punishment. There is the wife who says, "I don't like what you are doing, so there will be no sex tonight." The biblical concept, however, is that sex is a responsibility, not a favor, not a reward, and certainly not to be withheld as a punishment.

Paul gives the reason for this, saying, "The wife does not have authority over her own body, but the husband does, and likewise, the husband does not have authority over his own body, but the wife does" (1 Cor. 7:4). This statement declares that when you get married, you no longer have the authority or the right over your body. The moment you got married, your mate got the rights to your body.

I realize that this may sound unromantic and a bit blunt. The Bible recognizes that marriage should have affection and romance (see the Song of Solomon). Yet, beyond that, you need to realize that at the moment you were married, your mate received the rights over your body. This is true of both men and women. Verse 4 is careful to point out that the wife does not have authority over her body, and later, it says the same thing concerning the husband. This verse corrected the one-sidedness of the popular sentiment and public law of both Jews and Romans. The common idea of the day was that the wife was the mistress and the husband was the master, but throughout this passage, husbands and wives are treated equally.

Put verses 3 and 4 together. Verse 3 says that sex is a debt; verse 4 says that your mate has the right to collect. When you entered into marriage, you entered into a contract to pay a debt. You have no right to pay your debt only as the whim strikes you. Your mate has the right to determine the payment. That right is the Divine right to extract payment.

Someone will ask, "Is that absolute? Are there no exceptions? Can I say no at least once in a while?" The answer is, "Yes, you can say no." There is an exception. That's covered in the next verse.

Paul writes, "Do not deprive one another except with consent for a time that you may give yourselves to fasting and prayer. And come together again so that Satan does not tempt you because of your lack of self-control" (1 Cor. 7:5). The one exception to sexual relations in marriage is fasting. This exception has three requirements: 1) mutual consent, 2) a time limit, and 3) a spiritual purpose.

I know of a preacher who spends a week in a cabin alone with his Bible and the Lord once a year. That is the kind of spiritual purpose Paul is talking about. Frankly, this does not happen very often; it is an exception. The way this verse is written in Greek indicates that Paul had a skeptical tone when he said this. The Greek text indicates that Paul was saying something like, "If ... maybe ... the occasion ever arrives...." Then Paul immediately adds, "and come together again." The exception is just that, an exception and not the norm.

Please note that only one exception has been given. That means that all other reasons for saying no to your mate are not acceptable. To say I don't feel like it, or I'm tired, is not acceptable unless it is by mutual consent.

Paul gives the result of coming together. Namely, Satan will not be able to tempt you sexually. In other words, if you pay your marital debt, you will be helping to head off unfaithfulness. That's the point of the passage. Marriage prevents sexual sins, provided you pay your marital debt. Faithfulness prevents failure. Sexual adjustment prevents sexual sins. A good marriage protects a godly life.

Two practical principles in this passage head off unfaithfulness in our marriages. First, Paul says, "Do not deprive one another." The Greek word translated "deprive" means "defraud." This word was used of the misappropriation of funds. Refusal is robbery. Refusal is a crime and a sin!

Ladies, you probably have no idea what happens when you roll over and say no. It's not just a physical problem. For you to say no is a spiritual problem and it can create psychological pressure. Let me explain. A man is about ninety-nine percent ego. When his wife says no, his ego is defeated. That's the problem. When that is done repeatedly, many men feel an inner compulsion to go out and conquer some young beauty to build up their egos again. So when you say no, you disobey God and, perhaps, destroy your husband.

A second practical principle in this passage is that the married couple is to "come together again." The Greek term translated "come together" implies a "close fellowship and cooperation." The whole point of the passage is that you are to meet your mate's needs, so come together to cooperate to meet the other's needs.

Let's be specific. Wives need love. An old proverb says a man gives love to get sex, and a woman gives sex to get love. That's true. A woman views sex within the total relationship with her husband. She needs to feel that he loves her. If she does, it's easy for her to give herself to him, but if she ever feels like she is being used or "the only time he tells me he loves me is when he wants to go to bed," it he is not meeting her needs. She wants you to love *her*, not just *it*.

Sir, your wife needs touch. Another proverb says men are stimulated by sight and women are stimulated by touch. God has designed the female body in such a way that it is prepared for sex by foreplay, so she needs touch, tender touch, and loving caresses.

She also needs time. Women are not aroused as quickly as men (there are exceptions). That means men need to exercise self-control and take time. One Christian marriage counselor said that the average length of time for the sexual act in America is two-and-a-half to 5 minutes. He adds, "Forty-five million women are being cheated." There are more women raped in marriage than out of marriage because the husband does not give sufficient foreplay time for his wife's glands to function.

Ladies, you also need to cooperate with your husband. Remember the proverb which says men give love to get sex and women give sex to get love. Simply put, men need sex. As a rule, and there are exceptions, men need sex slightly more than women. Much of that is just plain physical. Men store up sperm and, after a while, have to have a release. So, men need sex. A sociologist studied Christians and asked, "How often would you like to have the experience if you could have it every time you wanted it?" Husbands' replies averaged every 2.7 days; wives' replies averaged every 3.2 days. A church lady told me she applied Proverbs 27:7 to this side of her marriage. That verse says, "A satisfied soul loathes the honeycomb, but to a hungry soul, every bitter thing is sweet."

Ladies, your husbands also need sight. The proverb says it well. Men are stimulated by sight and women by touch. That means you ought to be attractively dressed when he comes home and suggestively dressed in the bedroom when he goes to bed. If you don't have any suggestive negligees, you need to purchase at least one, and maybe several.

Ladies, your husband also needs an active partner. Even though he is stimulated by a sex drive and by sight, a passive partner will cause him to lose his enthusiasm. You ought to be actively involved in the process. If you don't know what I'm talking about, ask your husband.

Someone wrote Ann Landers saying, "With all the letters you've printed from husbands who complain about unresponsive wives, I decided a recent incident beats anything I've read so far. It doesn't require an answer, so please don't wrack your brain trying to come up with one. Last week, I climbed into bed with my wife after bowling a few more frames than I planned. I got home about midnight, kissed the little lady on the forehead (lightly) and accidentally brushed her leg with my hand. She turned over and mumbled, 'All right, go ahead—but don't wake me up.' How's that for a commentary on what some wives consider 'doing their duty.' I had a good laugh over it—maybe I should have cried. No, I did not risk waking the sleeping beauty. Her terms were not very enticing. Signed, that's the way it is at our house." Ann answered, "Yours and lots of others."

You might expect a chapter like this to end by suggesting you do your homework. That wouldn't be a flawed conclusion, but I would also like to suggest something else: you need to read a book. I know of a small paperback book written by a Christian that every married couple should read. I've given this book to many couples and many have returned saying that the book changed their sex life. I would suggest you read *Sexual Happiness in Marriage* by Herbert J. Miles.

Paul Newman had a reputation for being faithful to his wife. A reporter, reminding him that he surely had a lot of opportunities, asked why he remained faithful. Newman replied, "Why go out for hamburger when you have steak at home?"

CHAPTER 10

FAMILY FINANCES

A major problem in marriage is money. Do you worry about money? Most Americans do. One survey found that fifty-four percent of Americans worry about money. In marriage, worry is not the problem; war is. Do you and your mate fight over finances? Most couples do. One authority on the family has estimated that disagreements over money cause one-half of all divorces!

The issue is not how much you have or how much you make. Couples who are just beginning are strapped financially and struggle with the checkbook and so do couples who have more miles in their marriage and more money in their money market account.

Several years ago, a friend of mine, who at the time was a financial counselor for couples, told me of a case he had that involved a doctor and his wife. My friend began the session with the question, "What is the problem?" The wife immediately responded, "It's simple. We cannot live on the $180,000 a year he makes." The amount is not the issue. All struggle. Many fight over money.

Does the Bible offer help on the subject of family finances? The Bible says a little about family finances, but it has much to say about money in general, which should be applied to family money matters. So, while not many Bible passages speak directly to *family* finances, several give principles of money management that should be applied.

Honor the Lord

The Principle Proverbs 3:9 says, "Honor the Lord with your possessions and with the first fruits of all your increase." The Hebrew word translated "possessions" means "wealth." The phrase "first fruits" refers to the first portion of the crops, which the Mosaic Law says was to be given to the Lord (Ex. 23:19; Deut. 26:1-3). The Jews were to give the first part of their production, their earnings, to the Lord.

Those who did were blessed. Proverbs 3:10 states, "So your barns will be filled with plenty and your vats will overflow with new wine" (Prov. 3:10). Piety produces prosperity is a concept repeatedly taught throughout the Old Testament (Deut. 28:1-8; Mal. 3:10).

Application How should Proverbs 3:9-10 be applied? During the Old Testament dispensation, that verse meant that the Jews should give a tithe and God would bless them materially if they did. Applying it to this dispensation is difficult.

In the first place, tithing is conspicuous by its absence in the New Testament. Rather than tithing, the New Testament teaches proportionate giving, which implies the more you have, the more you should give (1 Cor. 16-1-4). While the New Testament does not guarantee material benefits for giving, it does say that you will be rewarded one way or another for it (Gal. 6:6-10).

Simply put, the principle is to honor the Lord and He will honor you (1 Sam. 2:30). Now the question is, "Do you honor the Lord with your checkbook?" Do you give to Him first, or does He get the leftovers?

A friend of mine tells me about selling junk. The fellow to whom he sold it gave him several twenty-dollar bills. When he got to church, it was all that he had on him, so he put in a twenty and thought to himself, "I'm giving the Lord my junk." That was not bad in his case because he regularly, faithfully, and proportionately gave to the Lord. Unfortunately, some people only give their junk to the Lord.

Save Some

The second principle to be applied to family finances is to save money. That concept is deeply rooted in American tradition. The question is, "Is it a biblical idea?" Some say, "No." No passage says save money. Furthermore, they say saving for the future contradicts Scripture because we are to trust the Lord for our daily bread.

Proverbs 6:6-8 Granted, no verse explicitly says save money, but Scripture does recognize the wisdom of the principle. Proverbs, the book of wisdom of the Bible, says, "Go to the ant, you sluggard! Consider his ways and be wise, which having no captain, overseer or ruler, provides her supplies in the summer and gathers her food in the harvest" (Prov. 6:6-8). Solomon sends the sluggard to the lowly ant to learn a valuable lesson of life. The ant, says Solomon, is wise in that even though it has no boss, it works. It is also wise because it prepares for the future by preparing food in the summer harvest and storing it for the winter. The ant saves in the present for the future. Writers have noted this characteristic of the ant since ancient times. One modern commentator points out that two different species of ants in the Holy Land lay up large stores of grain for the winter.

Proverbs 13:22 If there is any doubt that the Bible would permit a person to save and store up wealth, consider Proverbs 13:22, "A good man leaves an inheritance to his children's children." The application of this principle is to save money.

How much should a person, a family, save? The standard answer has traditionally been ten percent. If you can't save ten percent, at least save something and, as is practical, increase the amount until you reach ten percent. Someone has put it like this.

Can you find yourself here, now, or later?

> Age 21-30 I can't save now. I'm just getting my start in life. I don't make a lot yet. I'm entitled to a little fun while I'm young. There's plenty of time. Wait until I start making a little more, then I'll save.

> Age 30-45 I can't save now. I've got a growing family on my hands. Children and a house cost a lot of money. It takes all I have to keep them going. As soon as they're a little older, it will cost less; then I'll save.

Age 45-55 I can't save now. I've got two children in college. It's all I can do to pay their expenses. In fact, I had to borrow for their tuition last fall. This is the most expensive period in a man's life. I can't save a penny.

Age 55-65 I can't save now. I know I should, but things aren't breaking like they were. It's not easy for a man my age to step out and get a better job. I'll have to ride along where I am. Maybe something will break.

Age 65 I can't save now. We're living with my son and his wife. The Social Security check doesn't go very far. I wish I'd started saving twenty years ago, but it's too late now. You can't save when there's no income.

Provide for Your Family

The Principle The third principle is self-evident. It speaks about financially supporting a widowed mother or grandmother. Paul says, "But if anyone does not provide for his own, and especially those of his own household, he has denied the faith and is worse than an unbeliever" (1 Tim. 5:8). The phrase "those of his household" refers to a person's immediate family. One is to provide for and financially support his family.

Paul levels two charges against one who does not adequately provide for his family. First, he has denied the faith. What he is doing is contrary to the essence of Christianity. God, the Father, loves His family and provides for it. Not to do likewise is ungodly. Secondly, such a believer is worse than an unbeliever. Unbelievers, at least, take care of their own. Pagan reverence for ancestors is well-known.

The Application A prudent application of this principle includes budgeting one's income. The Greek word translated "provide" means "to foresee." Foresight and forethought are bound up in the essence of the word "provide." Gromacki writes that this verb "stresses the concept of thought beforehand." The believer must perceive the needs of the family and plan to meet those needs.

Every situation is different, but as a general rule, a family budget should look something like this.

The Lord	10%
Saving	10%
Housing	25%-30%
Food	15%
Clothing	5%
Medical	5%
Transportation	10%
Vacation/Recreation	5%
Miscellaneous	5%

The issue is not the high cost of living but the cost of high living. Calvin Coolidge said, "There is no dignity quite so impressive and no independence quite so important as living within your means." Or as Charles Dickens put it, "Income 20 shillings—expenditure 19 shillings, and 6 pence, result happiness. Income 20 shillings—expenditure 20 shillings and 6 pence, result misery."

Avoid Interest Payments

The Principle There is a fourth principle in the Scripture that, if applied, could save you a great deal of money. Simply put, as much as possible, avoid interest payments. Again, the Bible does not say that in so many words but recognizes the wisdom of it. In the Mosaic Law, God commanded, "You shall lend to many nations, but you shall not borrow" (Deut. 15:6; 28:12). Granted, the New Testament believer is not under the Old Testament Law (Rom. 6:14), and, therefore, this is not an absolute for today. Nevertheless, it is still true that "the rich rules over the poor and the borrower is servant to the lender" (Prov. 22:7). As the modern proverb says, "He that goes a borrowing, goes a-sorrowing."

The Clarification This truth can be misunderstood and misapplied. Borrowing is not morally wrong. In the Sermon on the Mount, Jesus said, "Give to him who asks you and from him who wants to borrow from you do not turn away" (Mt. 5:42). Had borrowing been a sin, Jesus indeed would not have said that. Yet, while borrowing is not wicked at the same time, we have seen that the Scripture recognizes it is unwise and should be avoided as much as possible.

In our society, people can't avoid credit entirely. If they did, they would probably never own a home, but excessive credit is like the fellow who said, "My wife thinks she is Teddy Roosevelt. She keeps running from store to store, yelling, 'Charge! Charge!'" Or the man who said, "My economic philosophy of life is middle of the road. I spent right and left." Excessive credit, and as much as possible, all credit should be eliminated. It may take time, years perhaps, but it can be done. Here's how I did it.

In college, I had several friends who got married, immediately got deeply into debt, and consequently had to drop out of school. As a result of watching their failure, I decided that when I got married, I would not get any credit at all, at least not until I finished school.

Upon college graduation, I married, moved to Dallas, Texas, and entered Dallas Seminary. For the next four years, I managed to avoid credit. In my last year in seminary, I decided having a gasoline credit card would be convenient. Thinking I had perfect credit, I applied to one of the major oil companies for a credit card, only to discover that I didn't have perfect credit—I had no credit at all! A member of my church who owned a service station came to my rescue and as a result, I obtained my first credit card.

From the beginning of my credit card experience, I pay them off *monthly,* avoiding any interest payments. However, to establish a credit rating, I did buy some furniture on time and eventually a house.

The day it dawned on me that credit and interest payments were expensive was when I bought my first car on time. I bought a year-old Chevrolet for $2,000 (inflation has taken its toll on the automobile!). The dealer gave me a $500 trade-in on my old Chevrolet, allowing me a balance of $1,500. The credit company gladly loaned me $1,500, but by the time I paid it back over three years, I'd paid them almost $2,000! Because I had to borrow the money, the car cost me nearly twenty-five percent more than its market value. I decided there had to be a better way. Then, I decided to eliminate credit from my life as much as possible.

To do that, I drove that Chevy until I had it paid off. Then, instead of trading cars, I continued to drive it. I continued to make car payments, but this time, I opened a savings account and made car payments myself. I planned to rebuild the Chevrolet until I had enough money in the bank to buy another car. A fender-bender, which was not my fault, interfered with those plans. The car was totaled, and I had no choice but to buy another. With the money I had in the bank, I still had to borrow $500 for the next car. This time, I took out a personal loan to be repaid in one year. That loan cost me a grand total of $30 (interest rates on car loans have also suffered from inflation!). I drove that car until I had enough money in the bank to buy my next one. I followed this practice through every car I have purchased since. I have bought cars without paying one nickel in interest.

I carry the standard credit cards in my wallet. I pay them all off every month, avoiding any interest payments. I also use the car plan for other major purchases. For example, if we need an item for furniture, I'll open a savings account and start making payments to myself. When I have enough money for the purchase, we buy that item, but not until we have the total price in the bank.

Look at the logic and the savings of such a plan: To keep it simple, suppose you bought a $100 suit and charged it to your credit card (I'm well aware that a good suit costs more than $100). If you took a year to pay it off, you would end up paying 18-21% interest, which means that you would pay $118-$121 for the suit.

On the other hand, if you put $100 in a savings account and made 6% or so on your money and then you bought the suit for $100, you would not only have saved the $18-$21 in interest, you could have made $6.00 besides. In other words, the borrower paid $118 for the suit you paid $94 for (you made $6.00 on your $100). The borrower paid 25% more for the suit than you did. (When I first began using this illustration, making 6% in a savings account was possible. Whatever the percentage, the point is the same.)

There are still more savings to be had by this plan. If you have the cash and are not a slave of a credit card, you can wait until the suit is on sale. A good sale would net you at least 10%, 25%, and as much as 40%. That $100 suit cost $75 and maybe even $60. If you paid $72 for a $100 suit, you would have paid 40% less for it than the one who purchased it on credit and ended up paying $120.

Be wise; avoid interest payments as much as possible.

Summary: The biblical principles of money management that should be applied to family finances include honoring the Lord, saving, providing for your family, and avoiding interest payments as much as possible.

If these suggestions were followed, your family would be better off because you would be saving for the future, your children would be better off because you would be providing a model for their responsibility, and your church would be better off because you would be giving regularly to it.

Family Finances

You're thinking, "I can't afford it." If you ever get started, you'll never miss it. The church in a rural area needed a treasurer. A businessman who managed the local grain elevator in town was selected. He agreed to take the job with two stipulations: 1) that no one ask for a report from him for a year, and 2) that no one asks him any questions.

The board debated the request, but they decided they would trust him for at least a year because he was such a devout, dedicated man. At the end of his first year, he said, "The church's indebtedness of $25,000 has been paid off. The church parsonage has been redecorated. Missionary giving has increased by 200%. The cash balance of $12,000 is in the bank and there are no outstanding bills."

The congregation was shocked and thrilled. They asked how such a financial boom had struck their church. He answered, "Most of you bring your grain to my elevator. As you did business with me, I withheld 10% on your behalf and gave it to the church in your name. You never missed it. Do you see what we could do for the Lord if we were all willing to give the first tithe to the Lord, who owns everything?

If you practice honoring the Lord and saving some, you will never miss it.

CHAPTER 11

HOW TO HANDLE MARITAL PROBLEMS

A young married couple decided to do some remodeling and redecorating. To save money, they did some of the work themselves. Together, they put up the paneling and laid the carpet. At the moment the carpet job was finished, the wife was out of the room. The husband, who had just finished the job, stood up, surveyed the situation, and smiled. Appreciated with the finished product, he reached for a cigarette. To his dismay, he discovered that his pack of cigarettes was not in his shirt pocket. He looked around the room only to discover a small lump in the middle of the floor. He realized the pack must have fallen from his pocket. It occurred to him that he would have to tear up the carpet to get the cigarettes.

An idea dawned. Looking around to make sure his wife would not see him, he stepped on the lump, twisting his shoe until the lump was flat. A few moments later, the wife returned. With his foot on the spot, he asked, "What do you think?" She said, "The carpet looks beautiful. Thanks." Then he asked, "Have you seen my cigarettes?" Without hesitation, she said, "Sure, they're on the window sill." Slowly, he turned his head. Sure enough, his cigarettes were sitting on the windowsill. Then she asked, "Have you seen our parakeet?" There will be lumps in your carpet; there will always be problems.

There will be problems after marriage. While dating, some couples buy the "fairy tale" about getting married and living happily ever after. Then, they get married only to discover one of the basic facts of life and marriage: that there are problems, problems, problems. Marriage is like a phone call in the middle of the night: there is a ring. Then you wake up.

There will be problems even after two married people have reached a degree of maturity. Some young couples have issues but think, "We're just getting started. After we're older, we'll grow out of these." The reality is there will be problems even after you mature, even after spiritual maturity.

A knowledgeable, mature, godly Christian leader once told me about an argument he and his wife had had over which tie he should wear. The two were college graduates with older children. They were mature adults and mature leaders in the Christian community on a national scale. Yet they were arguing over which tie he should wear. They never did agree. Finally, he decided he would wear the tie he wanted, regardless of what his wife said about it.

The reality is there will be problems in marriage. Shakespeare said, "The course of true love never runs smoothly" ("A Midsummer Night's Dream"). The question is, "How does a married couple handle marital problems?" For several helpful principles, consider Paul's instructions to husbands and wives in Colossians 3: "Wives, submit to your own husbands as is fitting in the Lord. Husbands, love your wives and do not be bitter toward them" (Col. 3:18-19).

Determine the Root Problem

When a problem arises in a marriage, the first thing you ought to do is determine the root problem. This is the first and foremost question you must ask. Sometimes, pinpointing the problem is half of the solution.

Sinfulness From a broad, biblical perspective, the individual is the root problem under every surface problem. According to the Scripture, all are sinners (Rom. 3:23). We are born separated from God.

Selfishness Out of our sinfulness grows our selfishness. We have dethroned God and enthroned ourselves.

So the real problem, my friend, is *you*. You want what you want when you want it. You do not want to yield to anyone else, not even God. It may not be too much to say that there is no such thing as a marital problem, but only a personal problem that marriage reveals. Marriage does not have problems; people do. Two root causes of an unhappy marriage are the man and the woman.

Bitterness When sinfulness and selfishness arise in a marriage, bitterness and resentment develop quickly. In Colossians 3:19, Paul exhorted husbands to love their wives and not be bitter against them. Of all the passages in the New Testament on the husband and wife relationship, the only one that mentions a sin between a husband and a wife is this one and the sin is bitterness.

The Ultimate In Marriage

I am personally amazed at how often resentment is at the bottom of marital difficulties.

Sociologists say that five problems regularly occur in marriage: money, sex, children, in-laws, and religion. I do not doubt that these five areas of conflict crop up in a marriage over and over again like weeds in a yard, but I question if any of these are the real problems. From a biblical point of view, it would be more accurate to say that these are the symptoms and the problem is *me*. The problem is not money; it is me. The difficulty is not sex; it is self.

Someone once wrote Ann Landers, "I hope your readers will learn from my bitter experience. Last week, my husband was driving home on slippery pavement. His car went out of control and hit a telephone pole. They called me from the hospital and said that he was in critical condition. When I arrived, my husband was in surgery, where he remained for almost two hours. I prayed the whole time. I was in the corridor when they brought him out. The doctor said that he had a good chance of recovering. Then, a nurse handed me his watch and billfold. Well, Ann, he has recovered, but I don't know if I ever will. In his billfold were two letters from a woman with whom he obviously had an affair. She was begging him to come back. I did not recognize her name and didn't know if she lives in this city or elsewhere since there was no envelope. I am crushed to think that my husband would have deceived me this way. Our twenty-two-year marriage was considered ideal by almost everyone who knew us. Yesterday, he asked for his billfold. When I handed it to him, he wanted to know if I had seen the contents. I said yes. He told me how horribly ashamed he was and he swore that he had not seen the woman since December and that he would never see her again. I'm trying to believe in him once more. I guess the real lesson to be learned here is this: Never carry anything with you that you would not be willing to let the whole world see. Lord only knows when the next of kin might be handed the damning evidence."

Signed, Victim of Fate

Ann replied, "How many of you could hand your wallet to your wife at this very moment and not be concerned about what she would find? If you can't, you'd better do something about it right now."

The problem is not the wallet but the person. This letter is typical of the way all too many look at the situation. They look at the circumstances instead of the center of the problem. They look at the symptoms instead of the disease.

Do Your Responsibility

Responsibility After you have decided that the real problem is your attitude and have identified what you must do to correct it, you need to determine to do your God-given responsibility. Colossians 3:18-19 spells out what your marital responsibilities are. Husbands are to love and wives are to submit. Love is the one word God wants every husband to remember in every situation. The one word God wants every wife to recall in every situation is submit. These are their respective responsibilities. A successful biblical marriage is one in which there is a responsible husband and a responsive wife.

Not Rights If you know anything about the Bible, you know your responsibility as a married partner. The problem is that we forget our responsibilities and focus on our rights.

The truth is every person has rights. There is no question about that. 1 Corinthians 7 spells that out in clear, unmistakable terms and indicates that a husband and wife have equal rights in a marriage.

You do not solve a problem in a marriage by demanding your rights. That only starts fights. More importantly, the Christian life is not a life of demanding rights. It is a life of learning to give up those rights. The Greek word translated "gentleness" in the New Testament contains the idea of yielding one's rights. If you want a *Christian* marriage, you have to practice the Christian virtue of giving in instead of standing up.

Not the Other's Responsibility If you are to handle your marriage problems biblically, you must determine *your* responsibility and not your mate's. Perhaps the worst thing a married person can do is say, "Remember what the Bible says," and quote the verse that applies to their mate. I don't know how often I've heard a wife say, "If he'd love me, I'd submit." That attitude is a direct violation of 1 Peter 3. Peter says that if your husband disobeys, the wife is to obey anyway. On the other hand, the husband often thinks, "If she'd submit, I'd love." Contrary to popular opinion, marriage is not a 50-50 proposition. It's a 100%-0 affair. Each partner should give 100% without demanding anything in return.

A wife telling her husband about his responsibility is like a child reminding his parents of their responsibility. A husband preaching to his wife about her responsibility is as out of place as an employee preaching to his employer about his responsibilities. Demanding submission is the world's way. Arrogant Adolph Hitler boasted when his bombs fell like rain upon London, "I will bomb the world into submission." The issue is not, "How can I make my mate better," but "How can I be a better mate?"

Depend on Your Resources

Depend on your resources to correct your attitude and your actions. Just before Paul gave these instructions for family living, he gave some commands for Christian living in general. If those general instructions for Christian living were followed, they would become the spiritual resource for living with others.

The Word For example, Paul says, "Let the word of Christ dwell in you richly in all wisdom, teaching and admonishing one another in psalms and hymns and spiritual songs, singing with grace in your hearts to the Lord" (Col. 3:16). Your mind is a vault, and God's Word is the currency. How is your bank balance? Are you rich or poor? Some marriages are bankrupt because they haven't made regular spiritual deposits; consequently, when hard times hit, they have no resources.

If you get bitter and dwell on a problem between the two of you all day, you will be cranky, cruel, and cutting. If the situation arises and you practice forgiveness and meditate in the Word of God, you'll be happy and your home will be harmonious. Warren Wiersbe has said, "If you plant the seed of the Word in the soil of the soul, you will reap the fruit of the Spirit."

Husbands, as head, you should take the lead. If you do, you will discover that a Christian woman listens to a man who listens to God.

To the Lord The other resource that Paul mentions in this passage is, "And whatever you do in word and deed, do all in the name of the Lord Jesus, giving thanks to God, the Father, through Him" (Col. 3:17). Later in this passage, Paul told Christian slaves, "and whatever you do, do it heartily as to the Lord and not to man" (Col. 3:23). Doing everything as unto the Lord is the key that unlocks the door to being a happily married person regardless of what the marriage situation is like.

Imagine a wife fixing a lovely dinner for her husband. As usual, he arrives late, and she is sure that he has stopped at the corner bar. While the dinner cools, she steams, growing more angry by the minute as she dwells on his apparent lack of concern for her feelings. By the time he walks in the door, she is ready to explode, which is precisely what she does. In the meantime, he has already erected his defenses and is quick to retaliate, "Why should I hurry home when all I hear is your complaining, ranting, and raving? I have to fortify myself for your barrage of insults." This prompts hysterics and bitter verbal lashes. Or she may turn cold and unresponsive, drawing into a resentful shell. It does not take many of these episodes before marriage turns completely sour.

Now imagine how the situation could be different. Let's begin with her preparing dinner for her husband. As a Christian in the right relationship with the Lord, she would not fix a dinner just for her husband. She would prepare it for the Lord, recognizing that what she is doing is God's will for her.

What happens when her husband fails to show up for dinner on time? Rather than fussing and fuming inside, she could have committed the meal, her feelings, and her husband to the Lord. She could have said, "Lord, I've fixed this dinner as unto You. I would like for my husband to be here to enjoy it, but he isn't. I have done what is pleasing to You and now my hopes for this evening are in Your hands. I am willing to accept Your will because I believe that You are in control."

If her thoughts during the evening ran along those biblical lines, then it is unlikely that she would meet her husband at the door with angry accusations. She would more likely respond with kindness and understanding. By breaking the usual bickering and battling pattern, she would channel those responses into a more constructive direction. Her husband may at first be surprised by his wife's new attitude and may even be suspicious, but if her attitude is genuinely consistent, he will automatically learn a new set of responses, whether or not they emanate from his relationship with Christ.

Summary: The way to handle marital problems is by performing your God-given responsibility as unto the Lord.

The Ultimate In Marriage

The non-Christian world's criteria for a successful marriage is whether or not two people make each other happy. The unspoken rule seems to be when one partner becomes unhappy, which is reason enough to dissolve the union. The Christian couple who uses this yardstick to measure their success is being led astray.

The reality is that the beginning of the end of the marriage is when each partner begins thinking in terms of "what I want my beloved to do to make me happy" instead of "what can I do to make my beloved happy?" What makes a honeymoon so delightful is that it is a time in life when we human beings are most likely to think and act unselfishly. Two people are gloriously happy as long as that unselfish atmosphere is mutually in operation. The pity is that the attitude is usually short-lived. God never intended it to be a passing mood. Frankly, happiness is not the goal of the marriage union any more than happiness should be the life objective of the child of God. Obedience to Jesus Christ should be the goal of the believer and obedience to Christ should be the mutual aim of married partners.

When a lady wrote to me to ask how to handle a marriage problem, I sent her a copy of this chapter on tape. Sometime later, she sent me the following letter.

> I'm writing to tell you that your message, "How to Handle Marriage Problems," has changed my life. I wrote asking for anything you had on love and marriage and you sent me the series on family living. I know that the Lord knew it was the right

time in my life to hear your message. I don't know how many women have learned from that tape what I've learned, but I feel the Lord has spoken to me personally through your message. I've been married for 31 years and my marriage has been full of problems. I've listened to many tapes on marriage. I heard messages on the role of the wife and husband that would tell you what they were and that self was the biggest hindrance, but they wouldn't tell you how you could solve the problem. I felt I was doing what I should and my husband, because he wasn't a Christian and was doing unchristian acts, that I had the right to get angry and *demand my rights*. You said in your tape this would create bitterness. BOY, WERE YOU RIGHT! The only thing I accomplished was bitterness and a bad attitude that created a fight. I acted like anything but a Christian. You gave an example of a wife fixing dinner and her husband was late because he stopped at Joe's Bar. That was my situation. I'm now trying to do all things as unto the Lord. I started this to see if I could get inner peace, not expecting a thing from my husband. I can't believe the difference it has made. It hasn't been long enough to really know what's going to happen, but the other night I scratched his back.

He's asked me to do this many times, but I never seemed to have time. I am now finding time and when he's late, my attitude has changed. I'm doing all things unto the Lord. The other night, he looked at me and said, "What's the matter with you lately?" (Praise the Lord!) I felt the same way about your message as I felt when I accepted the Lord. Everybody needs to hear this. After all, it will solve their marriage problems. Well, I got the same response as when I told people about salvation, except the people I had to listen to this message were Christians. They felt they would be giving up too much to try. They couldn't see that they were only giving up bitterness and resentment. Pastor Cocoris, I could go on and on for what that message has done for me. When you said, "Me, me, me" one of those "me's" finally got to me, and when you said, "Please, please listen," I finally listened.... The tape is priceless to me. Thank you for changing my marriage. I know it's the Lord that changed it, but he did it through you.

Signed, Your Happy Sister in Christ,
Mary Lou

CHAPTER 12
THE ULTIMATE

The essence of marriage is companionship, but The Ultimate In Marriage is Christ. The ultimate is not living in a palace on an island in the South Pacific with every creature comfort being attended to by natives. Jesus taught that life does not consist in the abundance of things one possesses (Lk. 12:15). Nor is the ultimate having a perfect partner. No such human exists! The ultimate is Christ.

The Ultimate In Marriage is a husband who loves his wife just as *Christ* loved the church and gave Himself for it (Ephesians 5:25), a wife who submits to her husband as to the *Lord* (Eph. 5:22), parents who bring up their children in the training and admonition of the *Lord* (Eph. 6:4), and children who obey their parents in the *Lord* (Eph. 6:1). In a Christ-saturated marriage, sex is not selfish; each partner is bent on satisfying his mate because that is what God said to do (1 Cor. 7:5) and which they quickly discover is the most satisfying kind of sex! In finances, the Christ-centered family discovers in their experience the reality of the truth that it is more blessed to give than to receive (Acts 20:35).

Striving to experience the ultimate in family living does not mean that there will not be conflicts or problems. There will be! It means the issues will be faced in a Christ-like and biblical manner.

Family members will learn forgiveness, faithfulness, compassion, and confrontation at home. Handled in a biblical fashion, problems produce a minimum amount of wear and tear on people. When Christ is installed in the center of "I" and "you," He prevents the "I" from being an egotist and the "you" from being a tool. When husband and wife desire Him more than each other and live for Him more than themselves, then and only then is there ultimate love, joy, and peace in their hearts and home. In such a house, the husband feels significant, the wife feels secure, the children feel loved and appreciated and Christ is glorified.

Someone will object that the picture I have just painted is idealism in the extreme. It is "pie in the sky," not a realistic "dessert" on the earth. "My husband isn't committed, my children are not convinced, the ultimate is not possible for me in this marriage," someone is sure to say.

Your home may not be experiencing the ultimate, but you can. Peter teaches that wives can "follow His steps" (1 Pet. 2:21) by being submissive to a disobedient husband (see "likewise" in 1 Pet. 3:1). Knowing Christ is knowing Him in the fellowship of His suffering (Phil. 3:10). Your suffering maybe your marriage, but you can still experience, even in a "bad" marriage, the ultimate in life because you can experience Christ in that situation. You can know Christ in your house. You can be an example to your out-of-it mate. You can be a testimony to your carnal children. You can be Christ-like regardless of your circumstances; that, my friend, is the ultimate! Paul was in prison facing death when he penned, "For me to live is Christ" (Phil. 1:21).

BIBLIOGRAPHY

Adams, Jay. *Christian Living in the Home*. New Jersey: Presbyterian and Reform Publishing Co., 1972.

Brenton, Myron. *The American Male*. London: George Allen and Unwin Ltd., 1966.

Colson, Charles. "BreakPoint" #020724, 07/24/2002.

Dobson, James. *Dare to Discipline*. Wheaton, Ill.: Tyndale House Publishers, 1970.

LaHaye, Tim and Beverly. *The Act of Marriage*. Grand Rapids: Zondervan, 1976.

Miles, Herbert J. *Sexual Happiness and Marriage*, Grand Rapids: Zondervan, 1987.

Robinson, Haddon W. "Without It, It's Not a Christian Marriage." *Good News Broadcaster*, November 1980.

Schlessinger, Laura. *The Proper Care and Feeding of Husbands*. New York: HarperCollins Publishers, 2004.

Plummer, Alfred. *A Critical and Exegetical Commentary on the Second Epistle of St. Paul to the Corinthians*. New York: Charles Scribner's Sons, 1915.

Wheat, Ed and Gaye. *Intended for Pleasure*. Old Tappan, New Jersey, Fleming H. Revell Company, 1977.

About The Author

G. Michael Cocoris is a gifted communicator. He can make even complicated subjects simple, clear, and practical. His breadth of experience has allowed him to relate to a wide range of audiences.

Michael received a Bachelor of Arts degree from Tennessee Temple University, a Master of Theology degree from Dallas Seminary, and a Doctorate of Divinity from Biola University. He traveled the United States for over a dozen years as a speaker. He has also been a seminary professor, visiting lecturer, and world traveler, including hosting tours to Israel and China.

Michael has pastored three churches, including a rural church when he was in seminary, an urban church, the historic Church of the Open Door, first in downtown Los Angeles and later in Glendora, California, and a suburban church, the Lindley Church in Tarzana California, a suburb of Los Angeles. While at the Church of Open Door, he had a daily radio broadcast.

Michael has written numerous magazine articles, mainly for *Biblical Research Monthly*. He has authored a number of books, including *Seventy Years on Hope Street, A History of the Church of the Open Door*; *How To Live A Biblical Spiritual Life*, *Clarifying the Confusion*; *Repentance, The Most Misunderstood Word in the Bible*; *Evangelism: A Biblical Approach*; *The Salvation Controversy*; *Lordship Salvation: Is It Biblical?*; *The Books of the Bible, the Subject, Structure, Situation, and Significant Verses of Each Book*; *Psalms, A Song for Every Situation, Each Summarized on One Page*; and *Counseling Theories, A Biblical Evaluation*. In addition, he was a contributor to The *NKJV Study Bible* and *Nelson's New Illustrated Bible Commentary*.

Michael is the pastor of the Lindley Church in Tarzana, California. He and his wife, Patricia, live in Santa Monica, California.